Musical Curiosities, Oddities and Liszts [sic]

The author. Drawn by his fourteen-year-old son, Benjamin. When I pointed out to Ben that he had incorrectly placed the long strings of the piano on the right of the piano, he responded: "Well, Dad, that's how it sounds."

Musical Curiosities, Oddities and Liszts [sic]

Arthur J. Lieb

Illustrations by Kim Borrego

The Squeezebox Press

BOULDER, COLORADO

Dedication

With the hope that they fall under the spell of great music, I dedicate this book to my grandchildren John (piano, sax, composition), Matthew (piano, trumpet), Ivan (the French language), and Vivien (piano).

I further dedicate this book to all of the wonderful music teachers I had: the elementary school teacher who taught "The Surrey with the Fringe on Top" to forty second graders for our world debut concert; to my instrument teachers, who despite constant nagging failed to get me to practice; and to my junior and senior high school and college teachers who introduced me to the vast repertoire of symphonic, chamber, and choral music that I love so much.

And to my love Kim who gladly indulges in attending three or four concerts a week with me.

Introduction & Acknowledgments

When I began going to concerts the whole experience was so formal: the musicians sat or stood on stage in their penguin suits. I was awed by the virtuosity. How could they possibly do the things they did? Like many of my high school classmates, I knew the Detroit Symphony Orchestra musicians' names like some of my neighbor kids knew the opening lineup of the Detroit Tigers. The difference was that Ronald Odmark played second oboe, not second base.

As my musical knowledge grew, so did my fascination with little-known facts. I learned that Mendelssohn wrote the "Overture" to *A Midsummer Night's Dream* when he was eighteen—perhaps the genesis of my fascination with the unusual, from the ridiculous to the sublime.

Serious writing and research for *Musical Oddities...* began in late 2016. While having coffee with James Bailey, then music curator for Boulder's Dairy Arts Center, I suggested a program of Darius Milhaud's String Quartets Nos. 14 and 15. These two quartets can be played together as Milhaud's Octet for double string quartet, op. 291, an extraordinary composition achievement. Jim asked what other "oddities" were out there and all I could think of was Mozart's *Table Music.* I immediately returned home and began searching the Internet. The results were neither disappointing nor modest in quantity. I began writing that moment.

There are more than two hundred compositions named in the following text. I had intended to footnote those which were available on the Internet. My task was made easier when I concluded that almost all of them are available, some even with films of performances. Check them out.

This is a book of total enjoyment. It is not meant to be read in one evening or even a week. It is full of information that will not make you rich, get you a promotion, or even make you smarter. But I do hope for some "wows," a chuckle, and a "boy, that is interesting."

Several friends and acquaintances provided information, anecdotes and stories from their musical experiences. To Bruce Galbraith, Kenneth Goldsmith, Anne Mischakoff Heiles, Robert Newkirk, Carter Pann, and Arnold Steinhardt, I am grateful.

I am especially grateful to ethnomusicologist Bruno Nettl. I met Dr. Nettl in the late 1950s when I was a junior in college. He was at the beginning of his distinguished career and serving as music librarian at my undergraduate school. He became a mentor and had a very influential role in my professional life. Sixty years later he still "mentors" me. I cannot thank him enough for his inspiration and friendship.

I am also grateful to James Bailey, Bill Elliott, Bruce Galbraith, and Patricia Johnson for reviewing and commenting on the text and to Marta and Bernd Wachter for helping me with Hungarian and German translations. And thanks to the staffs of the Boulder Public Library; the Howard B. Waltz Music Library, University of Colorado, Boulder; the New York Public Library for the Performing Arts; and the Music Division of the Library of Congress. Librarians are good people.

And hats off to pianist Charlie Cartier, singer-song writer, for permission to use a picture of him performing on Boulder's Pearl Street Mall. I could not imagine a better subject for my cover.

And thousands of thanks to editor Liz McCutcheon of As Told To and book designer Bonnie Mettler. Their professionalism, patience, and pleasant dispositions made it a pleasure to work with them. Their skills are in your hands.

Finally, I thank Kim Borrego for her wonderful line drawings that illustrate the book's text. Her imagination and understanding of the subject at hand is first class.

> Arthur J. Lieb
> Boulder, Colorado
> December 2017

The Beginnings

Music is the nearest at hand, the most orderly, the most delicate,
and the most perfect of all bodily pleasures;
it is also the only one which is equally helpful to all the ages of man.
—*John Ruskin,* Watson's Dictionary of Musical Quotations

Johann Sebastian Bach (1685–1750) was born in Eisenach in the duchy of Saxe-Eisenach. His was a family of established musicians, and his earliest music instruction came from his father and uncle. He was orphaned in 1694. A year later he moved to Ohrdruf, where his great uncle Johann Christoph Bach (1642–1703) lived and gave Bach his first organ lessons. Fantasia in C Major (BWV 570) for Organ, Bach's earliest known work, was composed between 1698 and 1704. At age eighteen Bach became court musician in Weimar, his first professional appointment.

Bach married his second cousin Maria Barbara Bach in 1707. They had seven children, three of whom died in the first year of life. Maria died in 1720. Less than two years later, Bach married singer Anna Magdalena Wilcken. In 1723 they had their first child, and in the next eighteen years Anna Magdalena bore twelve more. Only six lived beyond age four.

Bach composed 1,127 known works, an average of nearly twenty-two per year or two per month. This is quite an accomplishment considering that lighting was poor or non-existent and writing implements were crude. Houses were small, so there was lack of privacy. Add to that all those children running around the house!

His original manuscripts show staffs with precise parallel lines, but the staffs themselves are wavy, indicating that they were hand drawn with a rastrum, an implement with five nibs. Printed staff paper was available as early as the sixteenth century, but it was very expensive.

I examined the forty-six volumes of Bach's complete works. The collection requires five feet and four inches of book shelving. Based upon my unscientific samplings, I estimate 158 pages per inch of shelving and 100 measures of music per page, or 1,011,200 measures. If one copied a measure in thirty seconds, the task of simply copying Bach's music would take four years and two weeks to complete, working fifty-two weeks a year and forty hours each week.

Hänssler Classic music label released a 172-CD set of Bach's complete works in celebration of the composer's 250th birthday. The massive project contains over 175 hours of music—about four weeks and two days of listening, forty hours each week. It would require about seventy concerts, each lasting two and a half hours, to perform them all.

To quantify Bach's creative output, I compared it to other composers. Bach's published complete works occupy 5.6 cubic feet. The complete works of Franz Joseph Haydn, a very prolific composer, occupy 4.13 cubic feet. The works of Wolfgang Amadeus Mozart, whose lifespan was just more than half of Bach's, occupy 3.4 cubic feet. The complete works of Ludwig van Beethoven (1770–1827) occupy 3.1 cubic feet.

Bach died on July 28, 1750, in Leipzig. His last completed work is the magnificent Mass in B Minor. His remains are in the Thomaskirche, Leipzig, Germany. A large brass inscribed plate rests between the two sides of the choir, just at the foot of the altar sanctuary. A few years ago I sat just a few feet away, listening to a performance of one of his cantatas, thinking, "Thanks for wasting my time trying unsucessfully to learn the easiest of your Prelude and Fugues."

Study Bach: there you will find everything. —*Johannes Brahms*

Brass plate that covers Bach's grave in the Thomaskirche, Leipzig, Germany. Photo by the author.

The First American . . .

By the beginning of the twentieth century, music was enjoyed widely in the United States. *The Handbook of Musical Statistics* (Boston Musical Bureau), published in 1902, lists 529 musical clubs, societies, and organizations. Most of these were formed in the final decade of the nineteenth century. There were 39 in New York City, 11 in Boston, 20 in Pittsburgh, and 12 in Chicago.

. . . Orchestra

The oldest orchestra, the Philharmonic Society, was organized in New York City in 1842. Its first concert was on December 7, 1842, and was led by Ureli Corelli Hill. The program included Beethoven's Symphony No. 5. The St. Louis Symphony was the next orchestra formed, in 1880.

. . . Music Conservatory

The oldest music school dates to 1867 when the Boston Conservatory opened its doors. A century and a half later it continues to teach all orchestral instruments, conducting, piano, jazz, voice, and composition.

. . . Pipe Organ

The first pipe organ in a public place dates to 1713, when an instrument was willed to the King's Chapel by Thomas Brattle, a Boston merchant. A century later the Handel and Haydn Society held its first concert there in 1815. The Brattle organ is now in St. John's Episcopal Church in Portsmouth, New Hampshire.

. . . Piano Manufacturer

In 1896 the United States manufactured more than half of the world's production of pianos. The five largest piano manufactures were in the U.S. By 1909 three hundred manufacturers produced nearly 375,000 instruments. In 2016 the number of pianos sold totaled 30,795 as compared to 95,518 in 2005. (statistics.com)

Left, Pipe organ in St. Patrick's Cathedral, New York, New York. Photo by the author. *Right,* The White House piano, the 300,000th Steinway manufactured (1938) in the U.S. The author is at the keyboard. Photo by David Lieb.

One of the earliest American pianos is at the Historical Society of Pennsylvania. It is a 1789 square grand made by Albrecht & Company of Philadelphia.

You can tune a piano but you cannot tuna fish. Origin unknown.

... Composer

Francis Hopkinson (1737–1791) was a signer of the Declaration of Independence and is regarded as the first American composer. His 1759 composition is a song titled "My Days Have Been So Wondrous Free." Hopkinson's talents made him a true renaissance man. In addition to his musical talents, he was a jurist, artist, essayist, inventor, and designer of the American flag.

William Billings (1746–1800), the composer of works primarily for four-part a cappella chorus, deserves mention. Between 1770 and 1794 he published six hymnals. His most famous composition is the patriotic song "Chester." It was known to be sung during the Revolutionary War. Here is the third stanza:

When God inspir'd us for the fight,
Their ranks were broke, their lines were forc'd,
Their ships were Shatter'd in our sight,
Or swiftly driven from our Coast.

"Chester" is celebrated in *New England Triptych: Three Pieces for Orchestra after William Billings* (1956) by William Schuman (1910–1992).

. . . Opera

The first opera composed in the United States is *Aurelia the Vestal* (1841) by William Henry Fry (1813–1864). It awaits its premiere. Fry's *Leonora* was performed four years later and is believed to be the first American opera ever performed. The performance was at the Chestnut Street Theatre in Philadelphia on June 4, 1845.

The first opera composed in the United States with an American theme is *Rip Van Winkle: A Grand Romantic Opera in Three Acts* (1855) by George Frederick Bristow (1825–1898). Bristow was a child prodigy, joining the New York Philharmonic Society Orchestra at the age of seventeen. Eight years later he became concertmaster. *Rip* enjoyed a warm welcome and had initial run of over two weeks.

. . . Musical Comedy

George M. Cohan (1878–1942) is thought to be the first composer of an American musical comedy—*The Governor's Son* (1901). Three years later he introduced *Little Johnny Jones*, which included his great hits "Give My Regards to Broadway" and "The Yankee Doodle Boy." He wrote more than three hundred songs during his career.

. . . Music in Public Schools

Before the introduction of music in public schools, there were singing schools. The Boston Academy of Music was founded in 1832 and gave instruction in singing and music theory. The Cincinnati public schools began offering music in the curriculum about two decades later, led by Luther Whiting Mason. Mason wrote *National Music Course* (1870), an influential vehicle for the spread of music education.

Sadly, the end of the twentieth century brought a dramatic decline in teaching music in public schools. Music and fine art classes have virtually disappeared in many school systems. Politicians have stripped school budgets, forcing administrators to delete music and fine arts from the curriculum and denying students exposure to these important elements of culture. For a very long time I ended my e-mails with "I look forward to the day when music and arts programs in schools are funded and football teams have bake sales."

... First Published Music Book

Francis Hopkinson also enjoys the distinction of authoring the first music book published in the U.S., his *Collection of Plain Tunes with a Few from Anthems and Hymns* was printed by Benjamin Carr in 1763.

... First Radio and Television Broadcasts

The Chicago Symphony Orchestra performed in the first radio broadcast of an American orchestra in 1925. The next year the Boston Symphony Orchestra made its radio debut and the Boston Pops began regular broadcasts. The Philadelphia Orchestra made the first commercially sponsored radio broadcast in 1929.

The most famous radio broadcasts were of the NBC Symphony Orchestra led by Arturo Toscanini. They began in late 1937 and ended in 1954. From 1954 to 1963 "Symphony of the Air" made weekly broadcasts on NBC. Leopold Stokowski conducted. The Philadelphia Orchestra made the first televised broadcast on March 20, 1948, live on CBS from the stage of Philadelphia's Academy of Music.

The Metropolitan Opera began its national radio broadcasts of opera in 1931. Humperdinck's *Hänsel und Gretel* was the chosen work. Beginning in 1933, the Met's entire season was broadcast on Saturday afternoons.

Mozart war ein schmutziger alter Mann (Mozart Was a Dirty Old Man)

*Mozart's music is so pure and beautiful that I see it as
a reflection of the inner beauty of the universe.*
— *Albert Einstein*

I do not remember how old I was when I learned that I was born on the same day as Johannes Chrysostomus Wolfgangus Theophilus Mozart (1756–1791) (a.k.a. Wolfgang Amadeus)— January 27. Not knowing a note of his music, I somehow thought it something very special. In the mid-1960s a friend who was born in New Zealand explained how her parents moved from Austria to New Zealand in the mid-1930s to avoid religious persecution. I turned to her and said that I had visited Austria and reported the thrill of visiting Salzburg, Mozart's birthplace. I quickly added that the great composer and I shared a birthday. "What a coincidence," she responded. "So did my mother. *[pause]* But my mother was born in the very same apartment as Mozart."

K is for Köchel

Decades ago I read a biography of Mozart, and the author, whose name I do not recall, concluded that in a couple thousand years we may see another genius like Mozart. In spite of his short life, Mozart left us a huge catalog of music: forty-one numbered and twelve unnumbered symphonies, twenty-seven piano concertos, five violin concertos, seven concertos for woodwinds, four concertos for the French horn, thirty-six violin sonatas, twenty-three string quartets, eighteen masses, and twenty operas. An impressive output for someone who lived only thirty-six years! Six hundred and twenty-six compositions! After attempts by several chroniclers, Ludwig Alois Friedrich Ritter von Köchel, a nineteenth-century Austrian musicologist, writer, composer, and botanist, published *Köchel-Verzeichnis*, a list of Mozart works by date. "K.1a" is Mozart's Andante in C for Piano, written when he was five. Mozart's last work, although incomplete, is the Requiem Mass in

Mozart's Geburtshaus,
Salzburg, Austria.
Photo by the author.

D Minor, K. 626. Franz Xaver Süssmayr (1766–1803), Mozart's student, completed the mass in 1792.

Pre-Puberty

Between the ages of five and twelve, Mozart composed eighty-two pieces. Between ages six and eight, he composed his first eight violin sonatas, and he composed six more at the age of ten. His first four piano concertos were composed at age eleven, and the next year he wrote his Symphony No. 8 in D Major, K. 48.

Move Over Cage and Stockhausen

Chance music, more formally called aleatory music, seems like a twentieth-century invention. I immediately think of the modernists John Cage and Heinrich Stockhausen. But Mozart was way ahead of them. *Musikalisches Würfelspiel* means a musical dice game. Published posthumously, Mozart's K. 516f contains 176 two-part measures. A roll of dice determines which measures are used and in what order to produce a sixteen-measure waltz. The possibilities seem endless: 45,949,729,863,572,161 waltzes. If each waltz takes one minute to perform, it would take 1.5 million years to perform all of them, playing continuously, 24 hours a day. And no intermissions.

Mozart is sunshine. —Antonin Dvořák

Tsk, Tsk, Mozart

Epic Records released an LP in 1967 with a jacket cover showing a vacant lot strewn with the debris of a recent demolition. In the background is the wall of a neighboring building with the paint outlines of the rooms and stairways of its now non-existent neighbor. Playfully, someone whitewashed the album's title: *Mozart Is a Dirty Old Man — The Scatological Canons and Songs* on the wall. The English translations of the words are by Anne Grossman and include "Oh, You Earnest-Headed Donkey;" "Off to the Prater;" "Wine's a Refreshing Thing;" "Maiden, Turn Your Pretty Head;" "Kiss My Behind, Goethe!;" and "Lovey-Dovey, Where's My Glovey?" The album should be rated R: children under seventeen require an accompanying parent or guardian.

Table Music

Mozart's *Der Spiegel* (*The Mirror Duet* or *Table Music*) is a composition for two violins. It is written on a single page of sheet music (sixty-two measures), which is placed on a table with players standing at each end. One plays the piece from the top while the other plays it upside down and backwords. It works!

Mozart and the Pope

On a visit to Rome, Mozart and his father attended a performance of *Miserere mei, Deus* ("Have mercy on me, O God") by Gregorio Allegri (1582–1652) in the Vatican's Sistine Chapel. They returned to their hotel where Mozart wrote the score from memory, a six-minute work for two choirs (nine voices). Hiding the manuscript in his hat, he returned the next day to the chapel to "proof" it. His act was worthy of excommunication from the Catholic Church. *Miserere* was sacred and its music score or parts were not to leave the confines of the Sistine Chapel. It is unclear how Pope Clement XIV learned of this "sin," but Mozart was invited for an audience with the Pope, who praised the youth and conferred on him the Chivalric Order of the Golden Spur.

Mozart's Death

Mozart died on December 5, 1791, less than two months before his thirty-sixth birthday. Scholars have proposed many contradictory reasons for the cause of death, including homicide by the composer Antonio Salieri, Masons, or Jews. We may never know.

Emperor Joseph II: "Very many notes, my dear Mozart."
Mozart: "Exactly the necessary number, your Majesty."
An exchange after the premiere of *Die Entführung aus dem Serail*. (Watson Dictionary of Musical Quotations)

Trivia I

Who would believe that Ira Gershwin (1896–1983), lyricist for the classic songs "The Man I Love," "Summertime," and "Embraceable You," was a high school classmate of Yip Harburg (1896–1981) who wrote lyrics for the classic songs "Over the Rainbow," "It's Only a Paper Moon," and "April in Paris." The lyricists worked for their school newspaper and remained friends throughout their long lives. Their parents were Jewish immigrants from Russia. The Townsend Harris High School they attended was located in the borough of Queens in New York. Among its distinguished alumni are scientist Jonas Salk, editor Bennett Cerf, novelist Herman Wouk, Broadway composers Frank Loesser and Richard Rogers, actor Edward G. Robinson, congressman Adam Clayton Powell, and associate justice Felix Frankfurter.

Program Music

I could describe a knife and fork with music. —Richard Strauss

The New Grove Dictionary of Music and Musicians (2001) describes program music as "music that attempts to represent extra-musical concepts without resort to sung word." Program music has been around for a very long time. There are compositions from the Renaissance that sought to describe a thing or idea. Willi Apel's *Harvard Dictionary of Music* cites seventeenth-century French composer Marin Marais's *Le tableau de l'Operation de la Taille* as an example. The piece, for viola da gamba, describes a bladder surgery procedure.

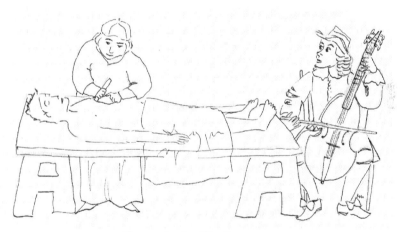

Illustration by Kim Borrego

The very popular four violin concertos by Antonio Vivaldi are collectively known as *The Four Seasons* (1723). There are currently over eighty known recordings of it. In the late 1960s Astor Piazzolla (1921–1992) wrote *The Four Seasons of Buenos Aires*, which is often programed with the Vivaldi. There is a ballet, *Seasons*, by Alexander Glazunov (1865–1936), and a violin concerto subtitled *The American Four Seasons* by American Philip Glass (1939—).

Tchaikovsky wrote a *Four Seasons, Op. 37*, for piano solo in twelve movements, one for each month. *The Seasons* (1947), a ballet by John Cage, was his first work for orchestra, choreographed by Merce Cunningham. It was performed that year by the Ballet Society (New York).

P.D.Q. Bach (a.k.a. Peter Schickele) wrote the oratorio *The Seasonings, S. 1 ½ tsp.*

American composer Carter Pann was named one of two 2016 Pulitzer Prize finalists for his *The Mechanics — Six from the Shop Floor* (2013), a sixteen-minute composition for saxophone quartet. The composer provided a description of the six movements that gives an insight into the compositional process of writing program music. The following are Pann's words:

I. "Hoist" is bold music that lifts itself upward and never falls down. The texture is very thick and replete with churning counterpoint.

II. "Drive Train" is fast music consisting of running eighth notes and quick turnabouts. It is almost always driving forward in a pseudo-Baroque frenzy.

III. "Belt (to S.R.)" is slower music set on a minimalist plain. As the movement matures the intervals get larger and the volume gets louder until a calm repose near the end. [The title's "S.R." is an abbreviation for American minimalist composer Steve Reich.]

IV. "Flywheel" is fast and angular jazz-jump music showcasing the baritone saxophone as a soloist accompanied by the other three players. When all four instruments come together in several places throughout the movement they play music that rolls forward on wheeling rhythms.

V. "Balance" is a slow, lyrical song. Every player takes the lead somewhere in this movement, singing beautifully over the texture. There are halted moments in this music that require the utmost balance in volume among all four saxophones together.

VI. "Trash" is straight-up turbo blues music. The theme upfront resembles that of a certain TV show from the '70s about a father/son garbage men duo. The music in the middle is more subdued call-and-response ragtime with a cheeky feel—all of it hanging on a texture of counterpoint about to boil over.

It would be so interesting to read Richard Strauss's words on how he would musically describe a knife and fork.

"All Aboard"

In my late youth, I discovered "modern" music and quickly fell in love with the dissonances and complex rhythms that my elders abhorred. The music of Arthur Honegger (1892–1955) attracted me very much. *Pacific 231* (1923)—a depiction of a steam locomotive beginning its journey from a standstill to full speed and back to rest—was especially enjoyable. There is a 1931 film by Soviet Mikhail Tsekhanovsky that uses the music. View it on YouTube. Another marvelous train trip is in *Bachianas Brasileiras No. 2*, by Heitor Villa-Lobos (1887–1959). Its second movement is titled "O trenzinho do caipira" ("The Little Train of the Caipira"). First class seating only!

Back in the U.S.A.

Popular program music with American themes includes Ferde Grofe's *Grand Canyon Suite* and William Schuman's *George Washington Bridge*.

The second movement of Charles Ives *Three Places in New England* is "Putnam's Camp, Redding Connecticut." It has two military bands marching into a common area, each playing a different march in a different key and with different rhythms and tempos.

Vivian Perlis, a biographer of Aaron Copland (1900–1990), tells the story about how people often approached the composer saying how they imagined him sitting isolated in a cabin in the Appalachian Mountains writing the *Appalachian Spring*. In fact, the famous ballet was originally titled *For Martha*. Martha Graham, its choreographer, gave it the title we know it by.

A Very Short Topical Liszt [sic] of Program Music

Insects

Rimsky-Korsakov: *Flight of the Bumble Bee*
Vaughan Williams: *The Wasps*
Bartok: *From the Dairy of a Fly*
George Crumb: Threnody III: *Night of the Electric Insects*

Animals

Vaughan Williams: *The Lark Ascending*
Sibelius: *Swan of Tuonela*
Debussy: *Poissons d'or*

Respighi: Gli Uccelli ("The Birds")
Hovhaness: *Bathing Fred the Cat*
Messiaen: *Catalogue d'oiseaux*
Dvořák: *The Wild Duck*
Delius: *On Hearing the First Cuckoo in Spring*
Caution: Benjamin Britten's opera *Albert Herring* is not about fish.

Death

Glazunov: *To the Memory of a Hero*
Richard Strauss: *Death and Transfiguration*
Liszt: *Héroïde funèbre* and *From the Cradle to the Grave*
Saint-Saëns: *Danse Macabre*
Rachmaninoff: *Isle of the Dead*

War

Beethoven: *Wellington's Victory*
Tchaikovsky: *1812 Overture*
Liszt: *Hunnenschlacht* ("The Battle of the Huns")
Gliere: *The Zaporozhy Cossacks* and *March of the Red Army*
Bernard Herrmann: *For the Fallen*
Ernest Schelling: *A Victory Ball*

Water

Smetana: *The Moldau*
Glazunov: *The Sea*
Debussy: *La Mer*
Virgil Thomson: *The Seine at Night*
John Alden Carpenter: *Sea Drift*
Lyadov: *The Enchanted Lake*
Respighi: *The Fountains of Rome*

Transportation

Leroy Anderson: *Sleigh Ride*
Liszt: *The Black Gondola*
Leopold Mozart: *Sleigh Ride*
Prokofiev: *Troika* from the *Lieutenant Kijé Suite*

Sports and Entertainment

Honegger: *Rugby*
Stravinsky: *Circus Polka for a Young Elephant*
Slonimsky: *Toy Balloon*

William Schuman: *Circus Overture*
Ernst Toch: *Circus*
Émile Waldteufel: *Skaters' Waltz*

Places

Sibelius: *Finlandia*
Richard Strauss: *An Alpine Symphony*
Liszt: *Hungaria*
Vaughan Williams: *Sinfonia Antarctic*
Ibert: *Escales* (Stopovers: Rome, Tunis, and Valencia)
Gershwin: *An American in Paris*
Hans Pfitzner: *Cracow Greetings*
Glazunov: *The Kremlin*
Karel Husa: Music for Prague
Mikhail Ippolitov-Ivanov: *Caucasian Sketches*
Borodin: *In the Steppes of Central Asia*
Enescu: *Rumanian Rhapsody*
Roy Harris: *Kentucky Spring*
Copland: *El Salón México*
Frederick Delius: *Florida Suite*
Ives: *Central Park in the Dark*

People, Real and Imagined

Richard Strauss: *Don Quixote, Domestic Symphony* and *Till Eulenspiegel's Merry Pranks*
Paul Dukas: *The Sorcerer's Apprentice*
Ernst Toch: *Pinocchio*
Malcolm Arnold: *Tam o'Shanter Overture*
Grofé: *Knute Rockne*

Celebrations

Grieg: *Wedding Day at Troldhaugen*
Arnold Bax: *Christmas Eve*
Respighi: *Roman Festivals*
Ives: *Decoration Day*
Copland: *Fanfare for a Common Man* (At a centennial celebration concert of Copland's birth, conductor Leonard Slatkin described *Fanfare* as our nation's second national anthem.)
Manuel Rosenthal: *Musique de Table* (An orchestra piece that describes the entry of the guests, an eel stew, garden vegetables,

a fruit basket, filet of beef, cheese, liquors, and after dinner cigars and conversation.)

Still More Seasons and Places into the Unknown

Delius: *Three Small Tone-Poems: 1. Summer, 2. Winter Night*, and *3. Spring Morning*

György Ligeti: *Atmosphere*

Prokofiev: *Winter Holiday*

Holst: *The Planets*

Michael Daugherty: *UFO:Traveling Music*

And let's not forget Frankie Valli and the Four Seasons.

Industry

Alexander Vasilyevich Mosolov: *Iron Foundry*

Carter Pann: *The Mechanics: Six from the Shop Floor*

Sensitive listeners to my Don Juan *can discern the color of hair of the amorous partners of the Spanish libertine, Don Juan.*
—Richard Strauss

National Anthems

Wikipedia lists 125 national anthems, the oldest being The Netherland's "Wilhelmus," adopted in 1568. The United Kingdom's "God Save the Queen," was adopted in 1745. When there is a gender change in the throne, the anthem's title changes appropriately. Fifty years later France adopted "La Marseillaise."

America's "The Star-Spangled Banner" has the words of Francis Scott Key written during the bombardment of Baltimore's Fort McHenry. It was set to a British tune composed by John Stafford Smith. It soon became a popular patriotic song and became the official national anthem in 1931. A congressional resolution passed on March 3, 1931, was signed by President Herbert Hoover.

The national anthem is not without controversy. Its wide range makes it very difficult for most people to sing, and there are four stanzas plus a fifth by Oliver Wendell Homes Sr. Many complain that its lyrics are too war like. Congress defined very specific behavior for its performance (36 U.S.C. § 30). Many performers have come under great criticism for their "versions," including Jimi Hendrix in his performance at the 1969 Woodstock concert, Jose Feliciano in 1968, the Dixie Chicks in 2003, and actress/comedian Roseanne Barr for her 1990 performance when she spat and grabbed her crotch at the end, imitating a baseball player.

Conductors of American orchestras have also found "The Star-Spangled Banner" troubling, but not for its wide vocal range. Their problem is with the harmonization. Antal Doráti, Stanisław Skrowaczewski, Eugene Ormandy, and Walter Damrosch all had their versions. Stravinsky reharmonized it and was warned by the Boston Police in 1940 that he could be arrested and subjected to a fine if it were performed.

Kindergarten—
Child Composers

Erich Wolfgang Korngold

Best known as a composer of film music, Erich Wolfgang Korngold (1897–1957) showed great talent at a very early age. Born in Brünn, Austria-Hungry, he was eleven when he composed the ballet The Snowman, which was performed in Vienna in 1910. It was followed by a piano sonata and two operas. The sonata was frequently performed by the great Artur Schnabel. The two operas, written in 1916, were produced in Munich that very same year, both conducted by Bruno Walter. Korngold moved to the United States in 1934 and began an illustrious career in Hollywood, where he produced sixteen film scores including music for *Captian Blood* (1935) and *The Adventures of Robin Hood* (1938).

The Mendelssohns—Fanny and Her Younger Brother Felix

Fanny Mendelssohn (1805–1847) was born in Hamburg, Germany. During her brief life she composed over four hundred compositions, mostly for piano and voice. Her teacher of composition was Carl Friedrich Zelter. Fanny was also a proficient pianist. Social attitudes prevented her compositions from being performed: she was a woman.

Fanny's little brother, Felix Mendelssohn (1809–1847), was born in Hamburg. He made his public debut as pianist at the age of nine. Between the ages of twelve and fourteen he composed twelve string symphonies, some of which are just beginning to get attention. At the age of sixteen he composed his Octet for Strings, and a year later his "Overture" to *A Midsummer Night's Dream*. Nearly two hundred years later these compositions remain high on music lovers' top-ten lists. They are absolute jewels and, coming from the pen of a teenager, unbelievable. From 1835 to 1847 Mendelssohn was the conductor of the Leipzig Gewandhaus Orchestra, where he introduced the compositions of Berlioz and Robert Schumann. He is also credited for a renaissance in the interest and performance of the music of J.S. Bach.

Georges Bizet

As a musician I tell you that if you were to suppress adultery, fanaticism, crime, evil and the supernatural, there would no longer be the means for writing one note. —Georges Bizet letter to Edmond Galabert

Georges Bizet (1838–1875), the composer of the opera *Carmen*, showed an early talent for music. Just before turning ten, he was admitted to the Paris Conservatory of Music where he studied theory and counterpoint, piano, and organ. He wrote his Symphony in C when he was seventeen.

Camille Saint-Saëns

The young Camille Saint-Saëns (1835–1921) began picking tunes on the piano and displayed perfect pitch at the age of three. A relative taught him the piano, and by the age of five, he was performing recitals. At ten he performed concertos by Mozart and Beethoven. At thirteen he was admitted to the Paris Conservatoire and began the study of the organ. Ten years later he became organist at the L'église de la Madeleine in Paris. His appointment there began a long succession of great organists, including Gabriel Faure and Henri Dallier. Although not his first composition, *Trois morceaux*, op. 1, was awarded first prize in a competition sponsored by the Société Sainte-Cécile in 1852. Saint-Saëns was seventeen years old.

"No Camille, you cannot go out to play. You must practice for another twenty minutes." Illustration by Kim Borrego.

Sergei Sergeyevich Prokofiev—a Precocious . . .

Sergei Prokofiev (1891—1953) started playing the piano at age three and wrote his first opera, *The Giant*, when he was nine. At age thirteen he was enrolled in the St. Petersburg Conservatory, studying with Anatoly Lyadov (1855–1914) and Nikolai Rimsky-Korsakov (1844–1908). About the same year, Prokofiev invented his own alphabet because he did not want others to know what he was writing in his diary. He graduated from the conservatory at the age of twenty-one and immediately entered into a piano competition. Performing his own Piano Concerto No. 1, op. 10 (1911), he walked away with the first prize. Two years later, he was commissioned to write a ballet for Diaghilev, but the score for *Ala i Lolli* was rejected. It became his *Scythian Suite.*

Recordings

Should we not fear this domestication of sound, the magic that anyone can bring from a disk at will? Will it not bring to waste the mysterious force of an art which one might have thought indestructible?
—Claude Debussy

How lucky we are to have recordings. Not only do they provide entertainment, they become documentation of events, poets reading their own works, concerts, and composers performing or conducting their own compositions. The Library of Congress's Motion Picture, Broadcasting, and Record Sound Division has over 3.6 million audio recordings in its collections.

My grandparents cranked their 78-rpm record player and changed its needle with some frequency. My parents had a 78-rpm player that had an automatic changer for ten- and twelve-inch disks. I got my first LP player while in high school in the mid-1950s. My children had a Walkman in the 1970s, and I got my first CD player in the early 1990s. My grandchildren get all of their music digitally on their iPhones or iPads. My current automobile can play CDs, and satellite radio service brings me every imaginable form of music. All of this progress in less than 150 years. What can be next?

Historical Landmarks of Recording

On February 19, 1878 U.S. Patent No. 200,521 was awarded to Thomas Alva Edison. His primitive reproducer of sound would create a revolution in the field of home entertainment and revolutionize the music industry. His early experiments began by transferring vibrations of sound onto paper and then tin foil. Cornetist Jules Levy was the first to record music, playing "Yankee Doodle." After experimentation by the Volta Laboratory a cardboard tube with a wax coating was invented. In the late-1880s, it was introduced with a machine to take dictation. The German American Emile Berliner was awarded U.S. Patent 546-586 on July 28, 1896, for a device that recorded on a disk. One of the earliest commercial cylinder recordings was a selection from Lehár's *Merry Widow* (1908). Two dozen years after Berliner and Eldridge Johnson founded the Victor Talking Machine Company, the company made its first electrical recording on March 21, 1925, pianist Alfred Cortot playing a Chopin *Impromptu*.

The recording industry made great leaps in the quality and durability of its products. In 1936 the German company BASF make the first-ever tape recording, Sir Thomas Beecham conducting the London Philharmonic. German Radio made the first stereo tape recording in 1942. The 33-rpm LP was commercially introduced in 1948 by Columbia Records. The following year, TCA Music Group introduced the 45-rpm, 7-inch, wide-hole disks and record changers. In 1954 two-track stereo tapes became commercially available, and the first stereo disks were released by Audio Fidelity four years later. They included performances by Johnny Puleo and his Harmonica Gang and the Lionel Hampton Orchestra. In 1963 Philips introduced compact cassettes, and a dozen years later Sony made cassettes portable with the introduction of the Walkman. Sony released the first CD player in 1982, the same year that Philips issued its first classical CD.

Other Interesting Notes about Recordings

Johannes Brahms made a wax cylinder of his Hungarian Dance No. 1 in 1889. In 1917 the Boston Symphony made its first acoustic recording for the Victor Talking Machine Company with Karl Muck conducting the finale of Tchaikovsky's Symphony No. 4. The first recording to sell more than one million copies was Enrico Caruso singing Leoncavallo's "Vesti la giubba" from the opera *Pagliacci*. It was in 1907.

Recorded Sound and Live Music

The growth of the recording industry and the sale of phonograph records eventually affected the employment of musicians. Juke boxes introduced in the 1930s replaced live music in restaurants and bars, and disk jockeys took to the air to broadcast the popular hits of the day. The American Federation of Musicians (AFM) took a strong stand by calling a strike on August 1, 1942, against all recording companies. Under the leadership of its president, James C. Petrillo, the union demanded that the companies pay royalties into a fund that would become known as the Music Performance Trust Fund. The record companies did not back down, and in spite of a ruling by the National Labor Relations Board and a personal plea from President Roosevelt, Petrillo refused to capitulate. In September 1943 Decca agreed to the union's terms. Thirteen months later RCA and Columbia caved.

And Speaking of Recordings

In 1987 the Oratorio Society of Washington and the Choral Arts Society were invited to join the National Symphony Orchestra for a recording of Mussorgsky's opera *Boris Godunov*. Led by Maestro Mstislav Rostropovich, the rehearsals and recording sessions were held at the Kennedy Center Concert Hall. Because the recording apparatus and booths for the soloists filled the stage, the chorus of nearly 250 singers occupied the front row seats of the audience section, watching the conductor on television monitors. Chorus members were expected to be at every rehearsal and every recording session. No exceptions. The project went on for about two weeks, and the daily schedule was never the same. For some this was inconvenient but not impossible. But for others a daytime session required taking the entire day off from work. One day the choir assembled at midday and was told that the session was cancelled and rescheduled. We later found out that a tenor soloist who was scheduled to record with us wanted to go to New York. The inconvenience to 250 chorus members was less important than the tenor's wants.

Sensory Marketing

Elevator music by Muzak provided soothing music for the ups and downs in life and made Kenny G a very rich saxophonist. Muzak reigned from 1954 until 2011, when it was purchased for $354 million. It has been replaced by sensory marketing, defined by Ari Brandt as a system that "empowers brands to forge emotional associations and connections with people through multi-sensory experiences such as sight, sound and touch, which solidify positive feelings, thoughts and opinions about a brand." For sight, think of the design and color of perfume bottles. For touch, think of a suede-like container.

A retailer of music service includes the following categories of its song lists: aggressive, bouncy, cheerful, cool, dramatic, dreamy, elegant, energetic, enthusiastic, fun, happy, intimate, laid-back, mellow, passionate, romantic, sexy, sophisticated, sweet, and warm. A claim is made that bars playing rock music sell more beer. I once played piano at a fine seafood restaurant in Rehoboth Beach, Delaware. It was always busy, and the owner would frequently ask me to play fast songs, saying that people would eat faster. I did not think so. If it did, it would be classified "turnover music."

Illustration by Kim Borrego

Anecdote I

Danny Pliskow, a lifelong Detroit friend, played with a Dixieland band at Greenfield Village, Henry Ford's collection of American historic buildings. The summer-long gig entailed playing on a flat-bed wagon drawn by horses. Michigan experienced record heat that summer. Danny reported to work one morning, only to hear an apology from the entertainment director. The musicians would have to play indoors that day because "the weather is just too hot for the horses."

Quizzes—Part I

1. Which American composer was born on the Fourth of July?
   a. Aaron Copland
   b. Leonard Bernstein
   c. George M. Cohen
   d. Steven Foster
   e. Edward McDowell

2. Who did not write five piano concerti?
   a. Ludwig van Beethoven
   b. Frédéric François Chopin
   c. Sergei Prokofiev
   d. Camille Saint-Saëns
   e. Heitor Villa-Lobos

3. Who wrote the text for Beethoven's "Ode to Joy" that is used in the final movement of his "Choral" Symphony?
   a. Johann Wolfgang von Goethe
   b. Heinrich Heine
   c. Friedrich Rüchert
   d. Johann Christoph Friedrich von Schiller

Answers can be found in Appendix 1

Composers and Musicians
with Handicaps

I shall hear in heaven. —Beethoven's last words

We all have heard about Ludwig van Beethoven's deafness, and people often ask how it was possible. What Beethoven did with music we do daily with written communication. No one hears the words they are writing. The words come from our heads and we transcribe them with pen or keyboard. Even the spelling just comes out. It is the same for music. We can all hear a musical theme in our heads. Musicians, through their training and practice, know that the distance from one note to the other is a particular interval (e.g., C to G is a fifth(C d e f G).

Give yourself a test. Without making an audible sound, listen to "Twinkle, Twinkle Little Star" in your head. A composer or a musician can take that mental song and transcribe it on paper like the following, but on a music staff.

CC GG AA G

FF EE DD C

GG FF EE D

GG FF EE D

CC GG AA G

FF EE DD C

Most composers create their compositions without the aid of a piano.

Beethoven's nine symphonies have a nearly fixed use of instrumentation—the standard strings, two each of flutes, oboes, clarinets, bassoons, French horns, trumpets, and trombones. In the Fifth Symphony (written when he was 60 percent deaf) Beethoven introduces a piccolo, contrabassoon, and three trombones. Those instruments were used again in the "Choral" Symphony, his last, together with bass drum, triangle, cymbals, four vocal soloists,

Beethoven and his hearing dog. Illustration by Kim Borrego.

and chorus, the timbre or tone color all familiar to him. By this time, 1824, he had been completely deaf for eight years.

Gabriel Fauré was deaf during the last two decades of his life, and during those years he composed thirty-six works. The Czech composer Bedřich Smetana lost his hearing for the last decade of his life yet continued to compose five operas, seven orchestral pieces, three chamber works, eight piano works, and five choral works.

Dame Evelyn Elizabeth Ann Glennie (1965–), the celebrated Scottish percussionist, regularly performs with major symphony orchestras, playing compositions written for her. She began to lose her hearing at the age of eight, and by twelve she had lost her hearing altogether. She performs in her bare feet, making it easier for her to "hear" the orchestra accompaniment.

During World War I, Austrian Paul Wittgenstein (1887–1961) received a gunshot to his right elbow and had his right arm amputated. After the war, he commissioned Benjamin Britten, Paul Hindemith, Erich Wolfgang Korngold, Sergei Prokofiev, and Maurice Ravel to write piano compositions for the left hand. A lesser known pianist, the Czech Otakar Hollmann, also suffered a right-hand injury during World War I. He commissioned Leoš Janáček, Bohuslav Martinů, and Erwin Schulhoff to compose works for him.

Of these works, Maurice Ravel's Concerto in D for the Left Hand is the most famous. It was composed in 1929–30, two years after Ravel began to lose his ability to speak or play the piano. Between 1927 and 1932, he composed seven works which included the Piano Concerto in G and the celebrated Boléro. He composed nothing in his last five years.

Denver's Slavens School (K-8) held its 2017 spring concert on the day that fifth-grade student Liam Wolf broke his right wrist. The fracture prohibited him from holding his trumpet. His father, Kurt, held his son's instrument while right handed Liam blew out some hot licks while fingering the valves with his non-dominant hand. The Show Must Go On!

Fifth-grade student Liam Wolf plays some hot licks while his father, Kurt, assists by holding the trumpet. Photo by the author.

Street Musicians
photos by the author

Krakow, Poland   Prague, Czech Republic

Jerusalem, Israel

India

St. Petersburg, Florida

Athens, Greece

Venice, Italy

Berlin, Germany

Trivia II

The American song composer Irving Berlin had a very different handicap. He could not read or write music: he hired a musical secretary to aid him. He was born in Russian in 1888 and immigrated to the United States in 1893. Unlike most American songwriters, he and Cole Porter wrote their own lyrics. I consider Berlin to be the ultimate American songwriter. Where else could an immigrant of Jewish heritage write the most popular Christmas song ("White Christmas"), Easter song ("Easter Parade"), and great and popular national song ("God Bless America")?

Acquaintance: "Ira, what come's first, the lyrics or the melody?" Ira (Gershwin): "The contract."

Music Written for
Non-Traditional Venues

Music in Flight

In the fall of 2013 I attended a performance of the *Helicopter String Quartet* (1995) by German composer Karlheinz Stockhausen (1928–2007) that opened the Venice Biennale International Festival of Contemporary Music. The performance of this composition requires the most unconventional venue: the fuselages of four helicopters.

I arrived at the Great Hall of Palazzo del Cinema about an hour before the scheduled performance. The parking lot next to the hall was cleared of all vehicles, and there sat four helicopters. About a dozen technicians were busy preparing for the performance. After some picture taking, I entered the hall and took my seat. Four large television screens were in the front. The members of the Arditti String Quartet walked on stage and acknowledged the audience's applause. They immediately exited the auditorium. Cameras captured the musicians boarding helicopters equipped with microphones, television cameras, and head phones to hear

Preparing for flight. Note the music score in the fuselage. Venice, Italy.
Photo by the author.

"Never, ever, be late for work!" Illustration by Kim Borrego

one another. The audience sat back and viewed the performance on four screens. When the vehicles landed, the four musicians and four pilots disembarked and took the stage in the auditorium for their bows. The performance took about twenty-two minutes.

After I returned to my hotel, I met a British couple and was invited to join them and another couple for dinner. I described the "Helicopter" performance. One of the diners asked me if I knew the British conductor Sir Thomas Beechen. I replied affirmatively, and he went on to say, "Someone once asked Beechen if he had ever conducted the music of Stockhausen. Beechen replied, 'No, but I have stepped in it frequently.'"

Life Jackets Can Be Found Underneath Your Seats

Water Music is a collection of orchestral movements composed by George Frideric Handel (1685–1759). It premiered in 1717 in response to King George I's request for a concert on the Thames. Its premiere performance is described in *The Daily Courant*, the first British daily newspaper: "At about 8 p.m. on Wednesday, 17 July 1717, King George I and several aristocrats boarded a royal barge at Whitehall Palace for an excursion up the Thames toward Chelsea. The rising tide propelled the barge upstream without rowing. Another barge, provided by the City of London, contained about fifty musicians who performed Handel's music. Many other Londoners also took to the river to hear the concert. On arriving at Chelsea, the King left his barge and returned to it at about eleven that evening for the return trip. The King was so pleased with the *Water Music* that he ordered it to be repeated at least three times, both on the trip upstream and on the return to Whitehall."

Regular or Decaf?

Bach composed his "Coffee Cantata" between 1732 and 1735, and it was first performed at Leipzig's Café Zimmermann, the site for the performance of many of his works. It is written for three voices: the narrator, Schlendrian, his daughter, Lieschen and a small instrument ensemble. It takes less than thirty minutes to perform.

Its German title is *Schweigt stille, plaudert nicht (Be Still, Stop Chattering)* and it is often performed as an opera. It is an eighteenth-century version of a parent-child conflict. Here is a glimpse of the libretto.

> **Schlendrian** *(the father)*
> You naughty child, you wild girl,
> ah! When will I achieve my goal:
> get rid of the coffee for my sake!
>
> **Lieschen** *(the daughter)*
> Father sir, but do not be so harsh!
> If I couldn't, three times a day,
> be allowed to drink my little cup of coffee,
> in my anguish I will turn into
> a shriveled-up roast goat.

Inner Tube Seating Is Available Only in the Deep End of the Pool

Steven Sondheim's first musical, *The Frogs*, was written in 1941 and first produced at Yale University's campus swimming pool. The book was a collaboration of Sondheim and Burt Shevelove. It was revived in 1974, again set at Yale's swimming pool, but this time with a cast of undergraduate swimmers acting as green amphibians. A 1990 London production was also set at a swimming pool.

The Arctic

With Norway's Wahlenbergbreen Glacier dominating the background, composer-pianist Ludovico Einaudi played his Elegy for the Arctic while floating on a platform boat. Dressed in black

Arctic ice. Photo by the author.

trousers and a black parka, the composer performed his near three-minute composition on a black Steinway grand piano. The sounds of flowing pieces of ice and occasional crashing of ice breaking off the glacier accompany the work. The composition was commissioned by Greenpeace. See it on slate.com.

Bargemusic

Since the late-1970s audiences have enjoyed chamber music on an 1899 100-foot steel barge that is docked in Brooklyn, about 500 feet from the Brooklyn Bridge. Bargemusic presents about 200 concerts annually. If you are in the Big Apple and want to attend a concert, you can take the "A" train, not Ellington's tune, but the MTA.

Photos by the author

Quizzes—Part II

4. What is the oldest American symphony orchestra?
   a. Boston Symphony Orchestra
   b. Chicago Symphony Orchestra
   c. National Symphony Orchestra (Washington, D.C.)
   d. New York Philharmonic
   e. St. Louis Symphony

5. Which composer lived the shortest life?
   a. George Bizet
   b. Lili Boulanger
   c. George Gershwin
   d. Wolfgang Amadeus Mozart
   e. Franz Schubert

6. Which composer lived the longest life?
   a. Irving Berlin
   b. Elliott Carter
   c. Henri Dutilleux
   d. Leo Ornstein
   e. Nicholas Slonimsky

Answers in Appendix 1

Music Museums

The world is filled with music museums. Some are dedicated to individuals and others are filled with music instruments, antique and modern. Here is a list of several unique museums:

American Jazz Museum (Kansas City, Missouri). In addition to jazz-inspired exhibits, the museum showcases the Blue Room, a jazz nightclub.

International Accordion Museum (Castelfidardo, Italy). Near the Adriatic coast, Castelfidardo is the home to several accordion builders. The museum exhibits over 150 accordions, and paintings, sculptures, and stamp collection with accordion topics. Replicas of historic accordion builders' workshops are also on display.

Musée de la Musique (Paris, France). Located the 19th arrondissement, its collections number over eight thousand items, of which half are musical instruments. Of particular interest are the saxophones and other instruments created by the Belgian Adolph Sax (1814–1894). Experience of the museum is heightened by audio devices playing samples of the instruments in excellent performances.

Museo del Violino (Stradivari Museum) (Cremona, Italy). Cremona is the birthplace of Antonio Stradivari (1644–1737), maker of the string instruments that bear his name. Three hundred years later many of these instruments command a price of over $40 million. The museum displays Stradivari's tools, models, and documents.

Museum Speelklok (Utrecht, Netherlands). The museum displays a most fantastic collection of mechanical music instruments, many of which are demonstrated. The collection includes music boxes, musical clocks, barrel and dancehall organs, and player pianos.

Musical Instruments Museum (Brussels, Belgium). The MIM has a collection of more than eight thousand instruments with emphasis on Belgian music history. Belgium was a major manufacture of eighteenth- and nineteenth-century recorders and the home of Adolphe Sax.

Phonoliszt Violina. A 1920 player piano with four violins that are played by a circular bow. The violins swivel so the correct string touches the bow and metal fingers press the strings for the note. It was all manufactured with early-twentieth-century engineering ingenuity. Museum Speelklok, Utrecht, Netherlands. Photo by the author.
See it perform at www.youtube.com/watch?v=RnzPMkJmyRc

Rose Museum (New York, New York). This museum illustrates the history of music performance at Carnegie Hall, a mecca for music lovers. Carnegie Hall, known for its great acoustics, was built in 1891 and opened with a concert conducted by Tchaikovsky. Programs, photographs, posters, and other memorabilia provide a capsule view of the master musicians who performed there. There is also a continuous video showing clips of many historical performances.

Other music museums worth visiting are: the **Mozart Wohnhaus** (Salzburg, Austria); the **Percy Grainger Museum** (Sydney, Australia); the **Scott Joplin House** (St. Louis, Missouri); the **Gershwin Room** at the Library of Congress (Washington, D.C.); the **Bela Bartok Memorial House** (Budapest, Hungary); the **Museum House of Arturo Toscanini** (Parma, Italy); and the **Sibelius Museum** (Turku, Finland).

Music Festivals

Aspen Music Festival (Aspen, Colorado). Taking place every summer for eight weeks, it presents about three hundred classical music events in a variety of venues. Many of the concerts are presented by excellent student orchestras.

Bard Music Festival (Annandale-on-Hudson, New York). The unique festival occurs during two long weekends in mid-August. Each year a different composer "and his world" is celebrated. There are eleven concerts, with pre-concert talks and panel discussions by musicians and scholars. The American Symphony Orchestra is the festival's resident ensemble. It is joined by fine soloists and chamber players. My favorite part of attending the festival is the ". . . and his world." Compositions of the featured composer's contemporaries, many which are very rarely performed, are included.

Bayreuther Festspiele (Bayreuth, Germany). Operas are performed during the summer in Bayreuth's Festpielhaus, an opera house that was built for Wagner operas. Its design and construction was supervised by the composer.

Architect Frank Gehry's Fisher Center for the Performing Arts, Bard College. The home of the Bard Music Festival. Photo by the author.

Cabaret Convention (New York, N.Y.). This annual October event has been sponsored by the Mabel Mercer Foundation since 1989. It hosts about forty cabaret artists in four consecutive evenings, "keeping alive the tradition of cabaret." Performances are held in the Rose Theater at Jazz at Lincoln Center. The artists are first-rate and so are the songs!

Festival dei Due Mondi (Spoleto, Italy). The festival takes place annually in June and July. It was founded in 1958 by the American composer Gian Carlo Menotti and features concerts, opera, dance, drama, and visual arts. A sister festival, **Spoleto Festival USA**, takes place from late-May to mid-June in Charleston, South Carolina.

Glimmerglass Festival (Cooperstown, N.Y.). Four operas are annually presented at this venue's main auditorium during July and August. Smaller works and recitals are performed in a separate facility.

Internazionale di Musica Contemporanea della Biennale di Venezia (Venice, Italy). Founded in 1930, this September festival takes place every two odd-numbered years along with the Biennale di Venezia.

Salzburger Festspiele (Salzburg, Austria). This annual festival may be the most famous in the world. Held in Mozart's hometown of Salzburg, it presents some of the world's most famous artists in symphonic and chamber music concerts and opera from mid-July through August.

Tanglewood Music Festival (Lenox, Massachusetts). This is the summer venue for the Boston Symphony Orchestra. In addition to symphonic music, there is chamber, choral, and contemporary music plus musical theater, jazz, and pop music.

Trivia III

We all know Charlie Chaplin as the zany character in silent and talking motion pictures, but few recognize his work as a composer. Like songwriter Irving Berlin, Chaplin did not know how to read or write music. Studios gave him musical secretaries, in the likes of David Raskin, to help him record his musical ideas. *City Lights* and *Modern Times* feature his music and are worth another view. His song "Smile" continues to be performed in the cabaret circuit.

Illustration by Kim Borrego

long [lawng] adj.;
antonym: short [shawrt] adj.

The Longest: A Test of Your Endurance

The uncontested longest music composition is John Cage's *Organ²/ASLSP (As Slow as Possible)* (1987). It is divided into nine sections, each taking seventy-one years to perform. A performance began in 2001 at the St. Burchardi church in Halberstadt, Germany. It is scheduled to end in 2640. Tickets may still be available.

If one does not have over six centuries to listen to the Cage work, try Richard Wagner's four operas collectively known as *Der Ring des Nibelungen*. Its fifteen-hour performance time is presented over four evenings, allowing plenty of time to stretch the legs between the long performances. Fans of *The Ring* are called "Ringers" and are known to travel the globe to see different productions. The pinnacle for a "Ringer" is to hear *The Ring* at Bayreuth's *Festpielhaus*. A travel agency recently advertised a package for *The Ring* and three additional operas at a cost of $16,300 per person, double occupancy. Caution: The price does not include transportation to and from Bayreuth. Start saving while young.

> *I sometime wonder which would be nicer—*
> *an opera without an interval, or an interval without an opera.*
> —Ernest Newman. Watson's Dictionary of Musical Quotations

The Life and Times of Joseph Stalin by Robert Wilson (1941–) is the longest known single opera. It lasts almost thirteen hours and twenty-five minutes.

If chamber music is your thing, you might want to attend a performance of Morton Feldman's String Quartet No. 2 (1983). It lasts a little over six hours, and the physical demand on the musicians is extraordinary. It was first written for the Kronos Quartet, but the quartet played only a shortened version in performance. In 1999 the FLUX Quartet performed the piece in its entirety. A

Illustration by Kim Borrego

Village Voice writer alluded to the possible use of catheters, but did not specify musicians or audience or both.

La Monte Young (1935–) wrote the six-hour *Well-Tuned Piano* in 1964. He waited for ten years before the piece received a performance.

The German-born British composer Max Richter (1966–) wrote *Sleep* (2016). He dubbed it his "personal lullaby for a frenetic world." It is intended to be listened to while sleeping. At its premiere audience members were dressed in pajamas and slept in sleeping bags and on camp beds. Doctors may wish to prescribe the piece to cure their patients' insomnia. The total performance is slightly over eight hours and twenty-four minutes. It is written for piano, organ, synthesizer, strings, and soprano. There are no lyrics; just vowel sounds.

Music of Short Duration

My search for short pieces of music was difficult. I immediately ruled out portions of longer compositions.

I distinctly remember my work in the late-1950s at radio station Detroit's WDET-FM. Its catalog of LP recordings included a file of titles by duration. The first card was a choral work by Arnold Schoenberg. *Wenn der schwer Gedrückte klagt (When the Sore Oppressed Complains)* (1905), a canon for four voices. Pierre Boulez's recorded performance takes forty-nine seconds.

The shortest opera I could identify is Darius Milhaud's *La délivrance de Thésée (The Deliverance of Theseus)* (1927). It lasts seven minutes and twenty-seven seconds.

Samuel Barber's *A Hand of Bridge* (1953) takes nine minutes to perform and *Hin und zurück* (1927) by Paul Hindemith is twelve minutes in length. The opera is an operatic palindrome, both in music and words. The plot opens with jealousy, murder, and then suicide. The libretto is then reversed and all is well that ends well (or at least better).

The manuscript is lost and so is the libretto, but it is believed that someone wrote an opera that takes two seconds to perform. It is in two acts. I spoke to a librarian at the Bibliotheca National and she too had heard of the lost work and added it was commonly believed that the first and only word of the first act was *taureau* (or bull). I plan to pursue this mystery. It would be interesting to know just how it ends. That's all folks!

The First Woodstock and the Tickets Were Scarce

In 1872 Johann Strauss Jr. visited the United States, specifically Boston. To meet public demand, a venue holding one hundred thousand was constructed. The concert was part of the World's Peace Jubilee and International Musical Festival. One thousand instrumentalists played and the orchestra was joined by a chorus of twenty thousand. Strauss's *Pizzicato Polka, Bouquet Quadrille, On the Beautiful Blue Danube,* and *Tales from the Vienna Woods* were on the program. The Waltz King was paid the astronomical sum of $20,000 for his appearance.

Trivia IV

The music school at the University of Colorado held a John Cage festival in 2012. One evening's performance included Cage's 4'33," a piece that is performed with the pianist sitting at the piano for that duration without playing a single note. During the performance the listener is supposed to be experiencing the sounds of the surrounding environment. Someone tapped me on the shoulder at the end of the concert. I turned and a man asked a question in much-fractured English, "Why man come stage play no music on piano?" I would have a difficult or impossible time explaining this to just about anyone, much less someone who barely spoke English.

I wonder if 4'33" is copyrightable. If I perform it will I have to pay royalties? What does the score look like? If I write a piece called 4'36" will I be charged with plagiarism?

Now that Mr. Cage's most successful opus is undoubtedly the delectable silent piece 4'33", we may expect his example to be followed by more and more silent pieces by younger composers who, in rapid escalation, will produce their silences with more and more varied and beguiling combinations . . . I only hope they turn out to be works of major length.
—Igor Stravinsky. *Themes and Episodes*

Political and National Leaders and Music

The Review Stops Here

On December 6, 1950, the Washington Post published a review of Margaret Truman's song recital. Ms. Truman was the president's daughter. The review was written by music critic Paul Hume:

> Margaret Truman, soprano, sang in Constitution Hall last night.
>
> It was not her first recital there, and it was probably not her last. Miss Truman is a unique American phenomenon with a pleasant voice of little size and fair quality. She is extremely attractive on stage . . .
>
> She is flat a good deal of the time—more last night than at any time we have heard her in the past years. There are few moments during her recital when one can relax and feel confident that she will make her goal, which is the end of the song . . .
>
> She communicates almost nothing of the music she presents . . . Yet the performance of music . . . was no more than a caricature of what it would be if sung by any one of a dozen artists today.

President Harry Truman responded to Hume with the following letter, hand written and signed on White House stationary:

> I've just read your lousy review of Margaret's concert. I've come to the conclusion that you are an "eight ulcer man on four ulcer pay." It seems to me that you are a frustrated old man who wishes he could have been successful. When you write such poppy-cock as was in the back section of the paper you work for it shows conclusively that you're off the beam and at least four of your ulcers are at work.
>
> Some day I hope to meet you. When that happens you'll need a new nose, a lot of beefsteak for black eyes, and perhaps

a supporter below! Pegler, a gutter snipe, is a gentleman alongside you. I hope you'll accept that statement as a worse insult than a reflection on your ancestry.

Just Fiddling Around

Former West Virginia Senator Robert Byrd was a lifelong accomplished fiddler, performing bluegrass music. Accompanied by three musicians, Byrd plays on an album called *U.S. Senator Robert C. Byrd; Mountain Fiddler.*

Secretary of Piano

Perhaps one of the most accomplished musicians who served in national public service is former Secretary of State Condoleezza Rice, the first African American woman to serve in that position. Rice is an accomplished concert pianist. At age fifteen she was soloist in a Mozart concerto with the Denver Symphony Orchestra. While serving in Washington, D.C., she frequently played with a quartet made up of attorneys. She has also performed with cellist Yo-Yo Ma and for Queen Elizabeth II.

A President at the Piano

President Richard Nixon made no secret about his piano playing, a talent that he took to the Jack Parr Show in 1963, two years after serving as vice president and nearly six years before his election to the presidency. He also played the saxophone, clarinet, accordion, and violin.

Need Not Worry Sonny Rollins

President William Jefferson Clinton enjoyed playing jazz (mostly blues) on a tenor saxophone. His saxophone can be seen at the Clinton Presidential Library, Little Rock, Arkansas.

Not for the Money

Alan Greenspan (1928–), former Chair of the Federal Reserve System, is a clarinet and saxophone player. He went to the Julliard School of Music in the mid-1940s to further his clarinet studies. Enthusiastic about jazz, he also attended the Musical Mart in the Bronx. According to Sebastian Mallaby's biography of Greenspan, teacher Bill Sheiner directed the youngster to sit next to another teenager, Stan Getz. Sitting next to Getz, Greenspan began to realize his limitations and wisely set out for a career in economics.

Oh, Give Me a Home

While governor of New York (1929–1932), Franklin Delano Roosevelt was asked what his favorite song was. In jest he answered "Home on the Range." That reply did not pay off very well; for the remainder of this life it was played wherever he went. I wonder how well he liked "Hail to the Chief"?

Other Figures and Their Instruments

Benjamin Franklin: violin, guitar, and harp
President Chester Arthur: banjo
President Thomas Jefferson: violin, cello, and clavichord
President John Quincy Adams: flute
President Woodrow Wilson: violin
Ross Perot: accordion
Patrick Henry: flute and fiddle
Sir Edward Heath, British Prime Minister: organ
Mahatma Gandhi: concertina

I only know two tunes. One of them is "Yankee Doodle"
and the other isn't. — Ulysses S. Grant

Anecdote II

"In the late 1960s, I frequently played in a low-stakes poker game with a number of other music professors at the University of Illinois, and a couple of times we were joined by a very distinguished visiting professor, John Cage. Cage was here to do a number of things but what received the most attention was a piece for six harpsichords and forty-eight loudspeakers with different sound sources titled HPSCHD. But Mr. Cage enjoyed getting together socially with some of the music profs who sympathized with his approaches, and that poker game was populated by some of these—musicologists Charles Hamm and Royal McDonald, composer Salvatore Martirano, music educationist Charlie Leonhard, jazz leader and new-music violist John Garvey. We played dealer's choice, including games with very odd names, some well-known and others obscure: 'Anaconda,' '23 and 32,' 'Buy-em-wild-if-paired,' 'Wild Shove-it,' and the most arcane, 'Hambone Two' (but there was no 'Hambone One').

You can see why John Cage might be attracted to these names if not the games themselves. He was a pleasant poker companion, although, when he said something, you didn't always know whether he meant it, or, caustically, the opposite. The point is, however, that Cage was not really an expert poker player and regarded the event mostly as a social occasion. And so he lost substantially—in that game (and don't forget the higher value of the dollar in those days), losing five dollars in an evening was something of a disaster. One day, Royal McDonald was a big winner, and Mr. Cage ended up owing him ten dollars, for which he wrote Royal a check. A year later, visiting Royal at his home, I saw that check in a small picture frame on his wall. He had decided, obviously, that owning this check was worth more than the ten dollars. 'What the heck,' Royal said, 'I can probably sell it for a thousand.' Unfortunately, Royal passed away at a young age a couple of years later, and I never found out what happened to that check, and whether his widow reaped the benefits." — Bruno Nettl, Professor Emeritus of Music and Anthropology, University of Illinois

"Shall We Dance?"
Ravel's Boléro

I have written a masterpiece. Unfortunately, there is no music in it.
—Maurice Ravel

Maurice Ravel wrote *Boléro* late in his life. It was completed in early October 1928 and received its premier performance the next month at the Paris' Palais Garnier by Les Ballets Ida Rubinstein. The New York Philharmonic, conducted by Arturo Toscanini, gave its U.S. premiere the same year.

The ballet scenario was suggested by a Goya painting. On stage was a large table in a tavern upon which "the principal dancer performed her convolutions while the men standing about the room were gradually aroused from apathy to a state of high excitement." Patrick Kavanaugh wrote that a woman shouted during its premier performance, "The composer is mad," to which Ravel responded, "She understood the piece."

Paris' Palais Garnier. The auditorium as
seen from the stage. Photo by the author.

In spite of the creator's opinion, *Boléro* grew to be Ravel's most popular work. It was first recorded in 1930. I stopped counting when the current number of recordings passed one hundred. The writer Nicholas Slonimsky said of the piece: "It was the first piece of serious music that penetrated the lower regions of musical culture."

Ravel arranged *Boléro* for two pianos. It has also been arranged for solo guitar, guitar quartet, four celli, brass ensemble, concert band, easy piano, and five-part (SATBB) chorus. There are also arrangements for brass, marimba, and saxophone ensembles.

Ray Conniff and Henri Mancini made popular recordings of *Boléro* in the mid-twentieth century, as did the pop groups Jefferson Airplane and Led Zeppelin two decades later. Ensemble Ukulollo (four ukuleles, percussions, and acoustic bass) has a video performance on YouTube. The Jack Loussier Trio (piano, bass, and drums) released a jazz version on Telarc. Add to that a recording by Johnny Paleo and His Harmonic Gang. If these aren't enough, the California performance artist Lun*na Menoh recorded it being played on sewing machines.

Yes, *Boléro* is popular!

Byproducts of Boléro

Steve Forster's drum pedagogy needs no explanation; its title says it all: *43 Binary Algorhythms Applied to Paradiddles Plus 43 Unique Exercises Based on Ravel's Boléro: A Compendium of Exercises Designed to Engage the Head and Hands of the Discriminating Snare Drummer.* A gift for the person who has everything.

For the person who needs (or wants) everything, consider purchasing a *Boléro* music box ($3,000), a jewelry box ($500), or a hand-cranked music box ($13), all available for sale on e-commerce.

Composers Who Were Inventors

Early Arms Race and an Unlikely Pair

Avant-garde composer George Antheil's autobiography is fittingly called *The Bad Boy of Music*. Hedy Eva Maria Kiesler is best known as the famous Austrian American actress Hedy Lamarr, who reigned on the silver screen for three decades. Who could have thought that they would invent a devise that would become the prototype to control torpedoes without detection or jamming? Their June 10, 1941, patent application (number US2292387A) called it the "Secret Communication System" and described it as follows:

> Our system as adapted for radio control of a remote craft, employs a pair of synchronous records, one at the transmitting station and one at the receiving station, which change the tuning of the transmitting and receiving apparatus from time to time, so that without knowledge of the records an enemy would be unable to determine at what frequency a controlling impulse would be sent. Furthermore, we contemplate employing records of the type used for many years in player pianos, and which consist of long rolls of paper having perforations variously positioned in a plurality of longitudinal rows along

Illustration by Kim Borrego

the records. In a conventional player piano record there may be 88 rows of perforations and in our system such a record would permit the use of 88 different carrier frequencies, from one to another of which both the transmitting and receiving station would be changed at intervals. Furthermore, records of the type described can be made of substantial length and may be driven slow or fast. This makes it possible for a pair of records, one at the transmitting station and one at the receiving station, to run for a length of time ample for the remote control of a device such as a torpedo.

Benjamin Franklin

Statesman Benjamin Franklin invented the armonica in 1761. Today that instrument is known as a glass harmonica. Any good piece of crystal will radiate a pure tone when rubbed with a moistened finger. Franklin took this result a step further by arranging a series of tuned glass bowls on a revolving rod. As the rod turned, the player would place a finger on a bowl to produce a sound. Franklin eliminated the need to moisten the performer's fingers by having the bowls rotate through a trough of water. While the instrument did not enjoy universal or extended fame, it attracted Mozart who wrote two compositions for it: Adagio in C, K. 617a and Adagio and Rondo for Glass Harmonica, Flute, Oboe, Viola, and Cello, K. 617. Both were written thirty years after Franklin's invention. Beethoven, Donizetti, Saint-Saëns, and Richard Strauss employed the instrument in one of their works.

A glass harmonica. Photo by the author.

The March King

John Philip Sousa (1854–1932) is best known for his more than one hundred marches but lesser known for his nine operettas. In the last decade of the nineteenth century, he and J.W. Pepper developed a bass tuba which we know today as the sousaphone, an indispensable instrument in marching bands.

The Stravigor

Igor Stravinsky (1882–1971) wrote short musical fragments on a blank sheets of paper as part of his composition method and created a device to produce a single or double staffs. It was derived from the commonly used nineteenth-century rostrum, a five-pointed pen.

Stravinsky called his devise "Stravigor." It is simply rollers housed on the ends of a rectangular box frame; one end has five rollers for a single staff and the opposite with ten rollers for double staffs. Embedded in the box is a pad which inks the rollers. Two caps that cover and protect the rollers make the device portable. Stravinsky was unsuccessful in gaining a patent.

An Anonymous Contribution

Patent application US5524638(A), by Paul Lyons, was for an "Amusement Device for Use during Sexual Intercourse." The website Change is Good describes it as "a condom with a little music-playing chip at the base that gets activated" during contact. Apparently one can program the choice of music. Possible selections: Gershwin's "Let's Do It Again," Roger and Hart's "Where or When," and Cole Porter's "Anything Goes." On the classic side there is Beethoven's "Appassionata" Sonata and an imaginary "The Rite of Offspring."

Trivia VI

Composers Felix Mendelssohn, George Gershwin, and Arnold Schoenberg, singers Enrico Caruso and Feodor Chaliapin and lyricist Ira Gershwin were all accomplished visual artists. The American painter Henry Botkin (1896—1983) was first cousin to George and Ira Gershwin. I met his niece in the 1990s, and she said her uncle once said that if George had not been a great composer, he would have been a great painter. Some people have it all! Self-portraits of the Gershwins and George's portrait of Arnold Schoenberg hang in the Gershwin Room at the Library of Congress.

Quizzes—Part III

7. "The Mighty Handful," a.k.a. "The Mighty Five," "The New Russian School," and "Могучая кучка," dominated Russian music during the mid-nineteenth century. Who was not a member of this group?
   a. Mily Balakirev
   b. Alexander Borodin
   c. César Cui
   d. Modeste Mussorgsky
   e. Nicolai Rimsky-Korsakov
   f. Peter Ilyich Tchaikovsky

8. Which of the following musicals had the longest run in America?
   a. Chorus Line (1975)
   b. Oklahoma (1943)
   c. Phantom of the Opera (1988)
   d. The Fantastics (1960)
   e. The Lion King (1997)

9. Ira Gershwin wrote lyrics for composers other than his brother, George. With which composer did he not collaborate?
   a. Kurt Weill
   b. Jerome Kern
   c. Harold Arlen
   d. Cole Porter

Answers can be found in Appendix 1

Trivia VII

To the Tune of Gershwin's "Let's Call the Whole
Thing Off"

You say Carmina,
I'll say Burana,
You say Burana,
I'll say Carmina,
Carmina, Burana,
Burana, Carmina,
Let's call the whole thing Orff.

SOBs (Sons of Bach)

"Kinder, seid ruhig! Koennt Ihr nicht sehen, dass ich arbeite?"
Illustration by Kim Borrego.

J.S. Bach came from a long line of musicians. One count lists fifty-three and it does not include his children. His family line ended in the mid-nineteenth century. With his two wives, Bach sired twenty children. Karl Phillip Emanuel and Johann Christian followed in their father's musical footsteps.

Mozart had six children, but only two lived to be adults. Franz Xavier Wolfgang Mozart (1791–1844), who incidentally was trained by Antonio Salieri, wrote songs and a piano concerto. Karl Thomas Mozart (1784–1858) became an official for the viceroy of Naples in Milan. Mozart had no grandchildren.

Dimitri Shostakovich had two children. Galina Shostakovich (1936–) became a pianist and biologist, and Maxim Shostakovich (1938–) became a pianist and accomplished conductor. Maxim's son, Dmitri Maximovich Shostakovich (1961–), is a pianist. Son and grandson have recorded the works of the patriarch genius.

Gabriel Prokofiev is the grandson of Sergei Prokofiev and is a composer living in London. He has composed violin, cello, and bass drum concertos, ballets, and orchestra and chamber music. He is known for combining classical and electronic music in his work. He also owns a nightclub called "Nonclassical" in East London.

Ernő Dohnányi (1877–1960) was born in Hungary and enjoyed a successful career as a composer and pianist, albeit a career that was interrupted by both world wars. His grandson, Christoph von Dohnányi (1929–), became a great twentieth-century conductor, serving in the capacity of music director of the Cleveland Orchestra from 1984 to 2002.

Imogene Holst (1907–1984) was the only child of the British composer Gustav Holst. She became a composer, arranger, conductor, and teacher. For years she worked for Benjamin Britten, and with him, became the driving force in the establishment of the summer Aldeburgh Festival in Suffolk, England.

Concertos for Neglected and Unusual Instruments

It is rare to hear a concerto played on an instrument other than a piano, violin, or a cello. Thanks to Mozart and Copland, you might hear a clarinet concerto, but rarely will you get to hear a concerto for a brass instrument, other winds, or percussion. But there are plenty of concertos for these and other instruments. Let us visit a few.

Morton Gould

American Morton Gould (1913–1996) created a most unusual concerto. His *Tap Dance Concerto* was premiered in 1962 by the Rochester (N.Y.) Orchestra, Danny Daniels, soloist. The work requires a small orchestra to allow space for the soloist. The composer integrates the tap dancing into the rhythmic part of the orchestra's texture, but allows the soloist to elaborate on the score's rhythmic patterns.

Performance May Require Assembly of Things Stored in Your Garage

The solo instrument is indefinable—a piece of garden hose, a metal eight-inch mouth funnel, and a French horn mouthpiece. That is what the British horn player Dennis Brain used to perform Leopold Mozart's Horn Concerto at the 1956 Gerald Hoffnung Music Festival Concert. Hoffnung was a cartoonist, musician, composer, and humorist. The liner notes of the recording renamed the piece *Concerto for Hose-Pipe and Strings*. When I first heard it, I was taken by how great a sound Brain got from the odd assemblage.

The Saxophone

In over six decades of attending orchestra concerts, I have never had the opportunity to hear a saxophone concerto performed. It is not for a lack of compositions or excellent players. The saxophone was invented in 1840, and in 1901 Debussy wrote his *Rapsodie pour*

Grave marker of Adolphe Sax. Montmartre Cemetery, Paris. Photo by the author.

Orchestre et Saxophone. Wikipedia lists eighty-three saxophone concertos with orchestra and forty-six more with concert band. There are also fourteen concertos for saxophone quartet and orchestra and six more with concert band. The virtuoso alto saxophonist Donald Sinta (1937–) told me there are more than two thousand concertos for the instrument. Sinta has spent his entire career teaching and performing and working to legitimize the instrument. During his lengthy career he premiered over forty works for the alto saxophone. A mighty accomplishment.

Larry Adler

The harmonica virtuoso Larry Adler (1914–2001) left his Baltimore birthplace as a youngster and found work in New York's vaudeville. By 1924 his celebrity earned him a role in a Hollywood movie. His popularity grew, but in the 1940s he became a victim of McCarthyism. Finding it impossible to work in America, he moved to England in 1952. Seven years later he began visiting the U.S. His musicianship was quite extraordinary and many respected composers wrote concertos for him, including Malcolm Arnold, Heitor Villa-Lobos, and Arthur Benjamin. I had the good fortune of hearing him perform at a 1990s Cabaret Convention at New York's Town Hall. After playing a few short pieces, he sat down at the piano and played his arrangement of Gershwin's *Rhapsody in Blue,* using his right hand to manage his harmonica and his left to accompany himself at the piano. Before leaving the stage he told the audience of his visit to Ira Gershwin who lay on his death bed. When Adler walked into the room, Ira looked up and said, "Penicillin, streptomycin, make a high ball, put some ice in."

Those Damned Accordions

It is rare to see an accordion on the stage with a symphony orchestra and even rarer to hear a concerto for accordion. It is a relatively new instrument, invented in 1829. Hindemith, Ives, and Shostakovich all incorporated accordions in their works. American John Serry Sr. (1915–2003) composed two concertos, Concerto for Free Bass Accordion (1964) and Concerto in C Major for Bassetti Accordion (1968).

> *Do you know that my very first experience as a composer was a concerto for accordion?* —Alfred Schnittke

National Instruments

The bagpipe is universally misunderstood as being Scottish. Its existence may go back to 1,000 BC, and its use is geographically widespread—Europe, northern Africa, and western Asia. There are rare instances that the pipes are used in an orchestra. One composition is the *Sinfonia with Bagpipe and Hurdy-Gurdy ("Peasant Wedding")* (1756) by Leopold Mozart. It employs a dulcimer, human whoops and whistles, and pistol shots.

Californian Kevin Weed (1962–) composed *Concerto for Highland Bagpipes and Orchestra* (1989) for the Orange County Symphony. It is in three movements: prologue; largo and march; and air and

Polish bagpipe,
Krakow Ethnic Museum.
Photo by the author.

jig. The composer, also a pianist and organist, was soloist. British composer and cellist Graham Waterhouse (1962–) composed a one movement *Chieftain's Salute* for great highland bagpipe and orchestra (1994).

> *I got to try the bagpipes. It was like trying to blow an octopus.*
> —Flutist James Galway, *An Autobiography*

The bandoneon is associated with Argentinean tango music ensembles, but it is also used in neighboring Uruguay and faraway Lithuania. In the latter it is used in folk music ensembles. The instrument was invented in the mid-1880s by the German instrument maker Heinrich Band and was originally intended for use in religious and popular music. In the later part of the nineteenth century it was imported into Argentina by Italian and German immigrants and became very popular. The Argentinean Astor Piazzolla (1921–1992) created the Concerto for Bandoneon and Guitar ("Tribute to Liège") in 1979. It was premiered at the Fifth International Liège Guitar Festival that year. Guitarist Cacho Tirao joined Piazzolla for the solo parts.

The eighteenth-century Austrian composer Johann Georg Albrechtsberger (c. 1736–1809) composed at least seven concertos for jaw harp and strings. The tooth-held instrument is also known as a Jew's harp, mouth harp, Ozark harp, or juice harp. It is one of the oldest instruments in the world. Chinese art dating to 400 BC pictures one. Because of the required grip by the teeth, the jaw harp has been referred to as "the orthodontist's best friend".

The alpenhorn is found in countries surrounding the Swiss Alps. It was used for communication, producing a sound that can be heard five miles away. The modern instrument can have a length of twelve feet. Leopold Mozart composed *Sinfonia Pastorella for Alpenhorn and Strings* (1755). More recently is Georg Friedrich Haas's Concerto Grosso No 1 for Four Alpenhorns and Orchestra (2013).

The Lower Depths

You can hear a bass oboe in Gustav Holst's *The Planets* (1914–1916) and works by Sir Michael Tippett, Frederick Delius, and Arnold Bax. The *East Coast Concerto for Bass Oboe and Orchestra* (1995) is a piece by Gavin Bryars (1943–) of Great Britain. A 1984 composition, *Survivor from Darmstadt*, by Robert Moran (1937–) is written for nine amplified bass oboes.

The contrabass flute is featured in a concerto called *Bantammer's Swing* (2008) by Ned McGowan (1970–). It had its premiere in Carnegie Hall. Two decades earlier Gunther Schuller's Contrabassoon Concerto received its premiere at the Kennedy Center. The National Symphony Orchestra's Lewis Lupnick was soloist.

Move over Tubby

Ralph Vaughan Williams provided a most melodic Tuba Concerto in F minor. It dates from 1954 and received its premiere performance by the London Symphony Orchestra, Sir John Barbirolli conducing. The soloist was Philip Catelinet.

Playing Around

There is a Concerto for Toy Pianos by Ryoko Amadee Goguen, a computer scientist at the University of California at San Diego. It received its premiere at the 2014 Toy Piano Festival in San Diego.

In 1948 John Cage wrote Suite for Toy Piano for *Diversion*, a ballet choreographed by his artistic partner, Merce Cunningham.

While not a concerto by name, Leroy Anderson's *The Typewriter* (1950) presents a solo typewriter and employs the percussive rhythm of the keystrokes, the typewriter bell, and carriage returns. It was written for the Boston Pops. I heard a U.S. military service band performance, and in the middle of the piece, the "typist" stopped abruptly, reached for the paper and "erased" something. The performance proceeded and the audience loved it. I am not sure how the current youth would react to this piece, not knowing what a typewriter actually looks like.

Beat, Beat Drums

I am surprised that orchestras do not perform more concertos for percussion. There is no lack of them and they are crowd pleasers. American Michael Daugherty (1954–) was commissioned by the Detroit Symphony Orchestra to compose a timpani concerto. It was premiered in 2003 with Brian Jones, soloist. A one-movement piece named *Raise the Roof* incorporates rock and roll and Latin rhythms and requires the timpanist to use foot pedals, and play an upside-down cymbal lying on a drumhead. Maracas, wire brushes, and the player's hands are used to strike the kettledrums' heads. Other American works for percussion and orchestra are by John Corigliano (1938–), Ned Rorem (1923–), Christopher Rouse (1949–), Steven Stucky (1949–2016) and Joan Tower (1938–), Philip Glass (1937–), and James Oliverio (c. 1960).

The Voice

Reinhold Glière (1875–1956) was born in Kiev, the son of a music instrument maker. His Concerto for Coloratura Soprano and Orchestra was written in 1943 for Devora Yakovlevna Pantofel-Nechetskaya. It is in two movements, an andante and scherzo. There is no text; the soloist chooses which vowel to use. *Concerto pour une Voix* (1969) is by French composer Saint-Preux (a.k.a. Christian Saint-Preux Langlade) (1950–).

I like an aria to fit a singer as perfectly as a well-tailored suit of clothes.
—W.A. Mozart

And One More

Visions & Fantasies: a Concerto for Ocarina and Orchestra was written by American Kristopher Maloy (1976–). It received its premiere in 2010 with soloist Carmen Hawkins. Another ocarina concerto of his was premiered in 2016 by the Washington Chamber Orchestra, Jenna Daum soloist.

The Growth of the Symphony Orchestra

In pre-Bolshevik times, a Russian Grand Duke was shown the layout of the Imperial Orchestra. "These are the first violins," explained the conductor, "and these are the second violins." "Second violins in the Imperial Orchestra?" exclaimed the Grand Duke. "All must be first!"
—Slonimsky, *A Thing or Two about Music.*

Symphony orchestras go back to the seventeenth century. That ensemble resembled what we commonly see in today's concert halls, but was considerably smaller. It included a string section of violins, violas, violoncellos, and double basses and a woodwind section of Baroque flutes, oboes, and bassoons. Its brass section had two natural horns and natural trumpets (instruments without valves). The orchestra might also have timpani and a keyboard instrument. Period paintings also show lute players.

Here are some significant dates in the orchestra's growth:

1607 Claudio Monteverdi writes for a harp in his opera *Orfeo.*

1681 The first recorded use of a flute is in a composition by Jean-Baptiste Lully (1632–1687).

1750 Johann Stamitz (1717–1757) introduces the clarinet and André Grétry (1741–1813) introduces cymbals in his opera *L'amitié à l'épreuve.*

1782 Mozart introduces the triangle and bass drum in his opera *Die Entführung aus dem Serail.*

1808 Beethoven introduces a piccolo, three trombones and contrabassoon in his Symphony No. 5.

1830 Berlioz introduces the E-flat clarinet (soprano clarinet) and the tuba in his *Symphonie Fantastique.*

1837 Berlioz scores his *Grande Messe des morts* (Requiem), op. 5, for a humongous orchestra—108 strings, 8 bassoons, 4 tubas, 10 timpanists playing 16 timpani, 10 pair of cymbals, a chorus of 210, and 4 brass choirs.

1872 One of the earliest uses of the saxophone is in Bizet's *L'Arlésienne*. A quartet of saxes is used in Richard Strauss's *Symphonia Domestica*, op. 53 (1903).

1874 The xylophone is first used in Camille Saint-Saëns's *Carnival of the Animals*.

1883 Tchaikovsky may be the first to use the accordion in a symphony orchestra. His Orchestral Suite No. 2 uses a quartet of them as does Prokofiev in his *Cantata for the 20th Anniversary of the October Revolution* (1936).

1891 The celesta was invented in 1886 and is first used in an orchestra in Tchaikovsky's first opera, *The Voyevoda*. The following year he gives the instrument a very prominent solo in the *Nutcracker Ballet*.

1912 The alto flute was developed in the 1890s, but its first significant use in an orchestra is in Ravel's *Daphnis et Chloé* (1912).

Major modern orchestras now employ about ninety musicians. For its 2016-17 concert season the New York Philharmonic employed ninety-five musicians; the Boston Symphony ninety-three; and the Los Angeles Philharmonic eighty-nine. That complement of musicians works well with the standard symphonic repertoire. For modern compositions, orchestras frequently hire additional percussionists, harpists, or other specialists.

Yes! We Have No Bananas

The Long Island Vegetable Orchestra was founded in 2011. An ensemble of 12 musicians performs jazz and classical music on instruments made of cucumbers, pumpkins, carrots and eggplants. If you are in Europe you might get to hear a similar group in Vienna or London. Give the LIVO a listen on YouTube.

Anecdote III

Arturo Toscanini (1867–1957) was the most celebrated conductor in the first half of the twentieth
century. But his celebrity was not limited to music
making; he was also known to have a violent
temper. I once heard a recording of a rehearsal.
He was preparing a concert aria and the tenor got
a fifteen-minute singing lesson from the maestro.
Then he began to take on the orchestra. Soon he
was yelling "bastards, bastards" at them in his
strong Italian accent. Eventually his voice faded
as he left the stage, accompanied by the sound of
music stands falling to the floor.

and IV

"Toscanini did break many a baton in his frustration in early rehearsals with the orchestra, and one landed on my dad's Stradivari, bouncing off the bridge. The maestro paled, jumped off the podium, and at once apologized profusely, expressing his concern about the violin. The bridge had saved the violin varnish from harm." The violinist was Mischa Mischakoff (1895–1981), concertmaster of the NBC Symphony Orchestra from 1937 to 1952. —Anne Mischakoff Heiles, violist, writer, and biographer of her father.

Bust (1924) of Arturo Toscanini by Adolfo Wildt.
Museo Nazionale Delle Arti. Rome. Photo by the author.

More on Pianos

A piano on display at Munich's Deutsches Museum.
Photo by the author.

Decorated piano, Staatliches Institut für Musikforschung, Berlin.
Photo by the author.

A piano made from a converted Yugo automobile. Union Station, Washington, D.C. 1995. The author is at the piano. Photo by Benjamin Lieb

Kennedy Center Concert Hall, Washington, D.C. 2000. A celebration of the 300th anniversary of the piano. The final concert featured an ensemble of ten pianos. It ended with a performance of the 1812 Overture. Instead of cannon shots for the finale, six stage hands fired toy cap guns. The performance was conducted by Leonard Slatkin. Photo by the author.

Piano with curved keyboard (1882). Music Instrument Museum, Brussels. Photo by the author

Siamese twin grand pianos. Musée de la Musique, Paris.
Photo by the author.

A tuxedo jacket. Paris men's shop.
Photo by the author.

Anecdote V

Robert Newkirk retired as principal cellist Kennedy Center Opera House Orchestra and professor of cello and chamber music, Catholic University, Washington, D.C. His career began in 1955 as a seventeen-year-old member of the Detroit Symphony Orchestra. While a student at the Curtis School of Music he was engaged to perform with the Casals Festival Orchestra for several seasons. Bob kindly supplied the following:

As an orchestra member I was allowed to attend rehearsals of the festival's chamber music ensembles. The Brahms Sextet, op. 18, was in rehearsal by the Budapest String Quartet, cellist Pablo Casals and violist Walter Trampler, when the electricity in the theater went off. Somehow, flashlights were produced and the observers were asked to hold the lights over the music. I was responsible for holding the light that would allow Maestro Casals to see his music. A press photographer repeatedly asked me to hold the flashlight more directly over Casals head and face in order to allow the photographer to achieve a clearer picture. I refused because I felt certain that the light would be too close to the maestro and impair his ability to concentrate and play freely, possibly disrupting the rehearsal. The photographer was quite upset with me, but I was convinced that I acted correctly.

On another occasion I had the opportunity to play the Prelude from Bach's Third Suite for Casals. That audition resulted in an invitation to study with him at the conclusion of the festival, which I did. The same photographer that I had given a hard time was taking pictures of me playing for Casals. I was not aware of this at the time. A few months after the festival, I received a package from that photographer which contained pictures taken during the festival. It included the picture of the rehearsal "by flashlight" and the audition. What a wonderful gift! I will forever be indebted.

Budapest String Quartet, Walter Trampler and Pablo Casals rehearsing by flashlight. 1958 Casals Music Festival, San Joan, Puerto Rico.

Robert Newkirk auditioning for Pablo Casals.
Photos courtesy of Robert Newkirk.

Jazz in Classical Music

Gershwin is the prince who has taken Cinderella by the hand and
openly proclaimed her a princess to the astonished world.
—Conductor Walter Damrosch at the premiere of the Concerto in F

Early Influences

Jazz is an American invention; it began with the vocal tradi-
tions of slavery, a reiteration and evolvement of the vocalization
of words brought from Africa. This tradition evolved in the nineteenth century into ragtime and blues, and eventually into jazz.
New Orleans gave birth to the genre, and jazz gradually worked
its way north to Kansas City and Chicago and eventually east to
New York. Our national boundaries did not hold a monopoly on
jazz; it soon spread to the European continent, especially during
World War I. Paris cafes and dance halls and Berlin's cabarets
began to swell with the American genre.

Jazz did not escape the ears of composers of classical music.
Contrary to a widely held opinion that Gershwin's *Rhapsody in
Blue* (1921) was the first to incorporate jazz, it was not. The earliest
I could identify is a 1917 composition by Paul Hindemith titled *The
Spleeny Mau*, written for flute, two violins, cello, double bass, and
piano. Unfortunately the manuscript is lost. In 1921 Hindemith
composed *Ragtime (wohltemperiert, a parodia of J.S. Bach Fugue)*, BWV
847, for orchestra. In between these works, Stravinsky composed
"Ragtime" *(L'Histoire du soldat)* (1918) and his *Piano-Rag-Music* for
player piano in 1919.

Darius Milhaud was introduced to jazz on a visit to the
United States in 1921 and explored New York City's jazz scene.
The following year he introduced his ballet *La création du monde*,
which has a very strong jazz influence. It is written for an
orchestra of seventeen: strings, winds, brass, and percussion. It
was commissioned by the Ballets Suédois, a dance company of
Swedes based in Paris.

The musician who invented swing ought to. —O.O. McIntyre

The next two significant jazz-infused classical compositions came from Maurice Ravel. His Piano Concerto in D for Left-Hand (1929–30) and Piano Concerto in G (1929–31) are both heavily endowed with jazz influences. Like Milhaud, Ravel had the experience of hearing jazz in the United States during his 1928 concert tour. Ravel met George Gershwin, and Gershwin supposedly asked Ravel about studying with him. Ravel's reply was, "Why would you want to be a second-rate Ravel when you can be a first-rate Gershwin?"

The Rhapsody

I think Gershwin's *Rhapsody in Blue* is the most iconic work in American classical music. It is a tour de force for the piano soloist, is filled with wonderful rhythms and harmonies, and is endowed with beautiful melodies. Gershwin composed *Rhapsody* for Paul Whiteman's *Experiment in Modern Music* at New York's Aeolian Hall on February 12, 1924. The composer performed the solo part. The concert also included works by pianist Zez Confrey (1895–1971), a *Suite of Serenades* by Victor Herbert, and *Chansonette* by Rudolph Friml. Also on the program were Irving Berlin's "Alexander's Rag Time Band," Edward McDowell's "To a Wild Rose," and Edgar Elgar's "Pomp and Circumstance."

Drummer Shelly Manne gave an interviewer his definition of jazz musicians: *"We never play the same way once."*

Two Great American Clarinetists

Benny Goodman and Woody Herman are the two great master jazz clarinetists of the twentieth century. Their fame leaped in the mid-1930s, and both performed until their deaths in the late 1980s. Just before his death, Herman played a concert with a small combo at the Smithsonian Institution in a series that honored early jazz masters. I attended the concert with my teenage sons. Herman opened the evening with his theme song, "Blue Flame." After the concert I said to my sons, "There is a great musician. When he played his theme song, it was probably for the umpteenth time in his career, but when he played it tonight, it was as if he was playing it for the very first time and just for us."

In 1945 Woody Herman commissioned Igor Stravinsky to write a solo piece for him. *Ebony Concerto* was premiered on March 25, 1946, at Carnegie Hall. The piece is scored for a "dance band" plus harp and French horn. Herman also commissioned Leonard Bernstein to write a solo piece for clarinet and big band. The result was *Prelude, Fugue, and Riffs* (1949), a piece that Herman never got to play. Its premiere was on a 1955 television program, *Omnibus*, Benny Goodman soloist. In 1950 Goodman premiered the work that Aaron Copland wrote for him, the Clarinet Concerto. It was first heard on an NBC Symphony Orchestra radio broadcast. Fritz Reiner conducted.

Americans do not deserve jazz. —Jazz trumpeter Dizzy Gillespie

Jazz Bands and Orchestra

Swiss composer Rolf Liebermann (1910–1999) is best known for his Concerto for Jazz Band and Symphony Orchestra (1954). It had its first performance at the Donaueschingen Festival of Contemporary Music (Baden-Baden, Germany), and its American premier with the Chicago Symphony Orchestra and the Sauter-Finnegan Orchestra, Fritz Reiner conducting.

Bill Russo (1928–2003) made his name in jazz while performing trombone in and making arrangements for the Stan Kenton Orchestra in the early 1950s. In 1968 his *Three Pieces for Blues Band and Symphony Orchestra* was premiered at the Ravinia Festival by the Chicago Symphony Orchestra and the Siegel-Schwall Band, a quartet of harmonica, guitar, drums, and string bass. The concert and a later recording by the San Francisco Symphony Orchestra was conducted by Seiji Ozawa. The harmonica of Corky Siegel dominates the twenty-two-minute work. Siegel's virtuosity is unbelievable.

In the early 1950s Edward Kennedy "Duke" Ellington (1899–1974) composed *Night Creature* for jazz band and symphony orchestra. The seventeen-minute work is in three movements, named "Blind Bug," "Stalking Monster," and "Dazzling Creature." The reception of *Night Creature* was lukewarm, and it took over a decade for it to be recorded on an album called *The Symphonic Ellington*. I was fortunate to attend a performance of it in the early 1960s in Detroit's Ford Auditorium. Ellington's band joined the

Detroit Symphony Orchestra, led by conductor Valter Poole. There was a robust series of improvised solos in one of the sections from members of the Ellington ensemble. They apparently got carried away, and I saw Poole madly flipping the pages of his orchestra score trying to find where next the symphony players would join the jazz ensemble. Months later Poole told me that he thought most of Ellington's men were inebriated.

The piano ain't got no wrong notes. —Thelonious Monk

Anecdote VI

During the big band era, many leaders, tired of paying royalties to the composers of songs they performed, began playing their own compositions. They also began naming their composition with amusing titles such as "Grandma, Cut Your Toenails, They're Rippin' the Sheets" and "You Stole My Wife, You Horse Thief!"

Anecdote VII

George Gershwin had the reputation of being a lady's man. While on tour he always had a piano installed in his hotel room. During an out of town tryout, he was attracted to one of the chorus girls and introduced himself, expressed his admiration for her looks, and told her that she had "inspired" him to write a song for her. He invited her to his hotel room so he could play it for her. And so he did. The next day the chorus girl was in the dressing room with the other dancers. While applying her makeup, she began humming the tune and was soon joined by all of the other dancers.

Music Censorship

The Catholic Church

Diabolus in Musica

A tritone is a music interval (the distance between two notes) of three whole steps. It is also known as an augmented fourth and the devil's interval. Think of the piano keyboard. Between each key is a half-step. If you start at middle C and go up two half-steps you come to D; then two half-steps from D to E; and two half-steps from E to F sharp (the first of three black keys below). A tritone beginning on C takes you to F sharp.

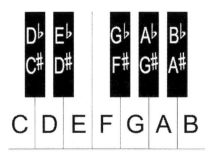

The Catholic Church fathers believed the tritone evil and referred to it as *Diabolus in Musica* (The Devil in Music). It was forbidden under canon law. The ban was reaffirmed in *Musicam Sacram* (1967), a document produced by the Second Vatican Ecumenical Council. It includes seven broad sections, including "General Norms," "Singing of the Divine Office," "Sacred Music in the Celebration of the Sacraments," and "Preparing Melodies for Vernacular Texts." Under these and other sections are a total of sixty-nine paragraphs describing accepted and unaccepted practices

Opera and the Church

In the beginning of the seventeenth century the performance of opera was forbidden by the Catholic Church during lent. In 1703 Pope Clement XI forbade all public opera performances for the sake of public morality. The ban was lifted in 1709.

The Third Reich

The Third Reich existed from 1933 until the end of World War II. Early on the government formed the Reich Music Chamber which was to govern what music was to be played and what music wasn't. The music of Jewish composers and atonal music was banned. The music of Bach, Beethoven, Brahms, Bruckner, Haydn, Mozart, and Wagner was promoted.

The *Reichsmusikprüfstelle* or Reich Music Examination Office was responsible for making sure that degenerate music was not performed. It published a newsletter listing compositions that were unacceptable, including the works of composers Irving Berlin and Fritz Kreisler. It specifically banned Franz Schubert's *Leise singt die Nachtigall,* Cole Porter's *You'll Never Know,* and Duke Ellington's *Caravan.* All jazz music was banned from performance.

The works of Felix Mendelssohn and Gustav Mahler, both Jews, were no longer played. Arnold Schoenberg, Oscar Strauss, Ernst Krenek, Erich Korngold, Paul Hindemith, and Kurt Weill emigrated to the United States. So did composers Bartok, Rachmaninov, Darius Milhaud, and Alma Mahler.

Music under Mao: China's Great Proletarian Cultural Revolution

Simply put, music under Mao Tse-tung was a tool for propaganda. Western music was banned and the instruments used to play the music were destroyed. Even traditional Chinese music took a hit. On a trip to China I visited with a string bassist, a member the Beijing Radio Orchestra. He told me that as a young musician in the mid-1960s he was employed in a symphony orchestra and enjoyed a modest living. The organization was dismantled and his bass was confiscated. Western music regained status in the 1980s, and he was hired to perform for live performances and broadcasts. His great problem was the difficulty of acquiring a decent instrument.

Things have radically changed. Western classical music is now widely performed, and in Beijing there is a beautiful new National Centre for the Performing Arts that opened in 2007. Its three halls—opera, music, and theater—are architecturally magnificent. It was designed by the French architect Paul Andreu. Beijing now has three symphony orchestras, as does Shanghai.

Советский союз (The Soviet Union)

In 2008 I attended the Bard Music Festival in New York's Hudson Valley. The theme was Prokofiev and His World. Proceeding the two long weekends of concerts was the world premiere of Prokofiev's ballet, *Romeo and Juliet* (1935). How was it possible that it took over seventy-five years to premiere this work? Two words— Josef Stalin. During the preparation of the festival, a researcher in Moscow found the original score to what is perhaps the most popular of Prokofiev's work. The original score never saw the light of day because it had a happy ending, and Josef Stalin, General Secretary of the Central Committee of the Communist Party of the Soviet Union, forbade its performance. Prokofiev argued, without success, that dead people could not dance. He lost, and for nearly three-quarters of a century ballet lovers saw or heard only his revised score.

Censorship. Illustration by Kim Borrego.

Stalin never lost his grip. In 1936 he attended a Bolshoi Theatre production of Dmitri Shostakovich's *Lady Macbeth of Mtsensk*. Another musical expulsion. Soon the government clampdown widened. Composers Sergei Prokofiev, Aram Khachaturian, Nikolai Myaskovsky, and others were denied their creative freedom. Socialist realism became the norm. Many composers folded. Others continued their creative efforts, but performances were denied.

Things relaxed during World War II, but in 1948 the Central Committee of the Communist Party issued a decree:

(1) To condemn the formalist tendency in Soviet Music as being anti-People and leading to the liquidation of music.

(2) To propose to the Propaganda and Agitation Department of the Central Committee of the C.P.S.U. and to the Government Art Committee that they take the necessary steps for improving the state of affairs in Soviet Music, and liquidate the faults enumerated to the present decree.

(3) To call upon Soviet composers to become more conscious of their duties to the Soviet people . . . and assure a great upsurge of creative activity which would lead to the creation of high-quality works worthy of the Soviet people." (Alexander Werth, *Musical Uproar in Moscow*).

The heat was on again.

Sculpture of Mstislav Rostropovich, Checkpoint Charlie Museum, Berlin. On November 11, 1989, the Berlin wall was opened, and two days later Rostropovich flew to the city and played Bach's Cello Suites, in the shadow of the graffiti covered Wall. Photo by the author.

I remember speaking to my undergraduate advisor and asking, "How is it that Shostakovich's music is banned in the U.S.S.R. but a recording of his most recent symphony was just released by the Philadelphia Orchestra?" No answer was forthcoming, but decades later I leaned that the great Soviet cellist, Mstislav "Slava" Rostropovich, who had access to the West, would stash a few pages of a new Shostakovich score into his luggage. Eventually the whole composition was outside the U.S.S.R. The parts were created and a recording evolved.

On October 31, 1970, Rostropovich sent a very long open letter to *Pravda*, a letter very critical of the Soviet government and its control over the arts. It was not published except in the West. The following paragraph well represents the tone of the letter:

> Every person must have the right to think and express views fearlessly and independently about things that are known to him, that he has personally thought out and lived through—and not simply to offer weak variations on an OPIN-ION implanted in him. It is our duty to arrive at free discussion without prompting or rebuffs.

Soon the passports of Rostropovich and his wife, the prima donna Galina Vishnevskaya, were confiscated. In 1974 their passports were returned and they moved to the United States. In 1977 Rostropovich became music director of the National Symphony Orchestra in Washington, D.C. Early in 1978 the Soviet government stripped the couple of their citizenship.

In May 1979 I joined the Oratorio Society of Washington. My first engagement with the OSW was a Fourth of July concert on the Nation's Mall. We performed Randall Thompson's *Testimony of Freedom* with the National Symphony Orchestra, Mstislav "Slava" Rostropovich conducting. The Thompson work uses words of Thomas Jefferson and the opening line is "The God who gave us life gave us liberty at the same time." A crowd of more than sixty thousand attended that concert. Standing in a temporary music shell facing the west side of the U.S. Capitol, I sang those words as tears flowed down my cheeks. I cannot remember ever feeling in better company then Slava's. After the concert I stood behind the stage to view the fireworks display. Rostropovich stood at my left, only a few feet away, holding a beer in his hand and watching the amazing pyrotechnics cascade over and around the Washington Monument. I wondered just what he was thinking.

Rostropovich died on April 27, 2007, just days before I departed for a visit to Russia. He was interred in the Novodevichy Cemetery in Moscow. On the last day in Moscow we visited the cemetery. I rushed off the tour bus and entered the grounds that hold the remains of many of famous Russians, including Prokofiev and Shostakovich. In front of me was a crowd of several hundred people and I could hear a male choir singing liturgical music. I was curious and made my way through the huddled mourners. When I got to the front, I found myself standing at Rostropovich's grave. His widow and two daughters stood just a few feet to my left. It was the ninth day after his death, a significant day of mourning for Eastern Orthodox Christians. I felt very, very privileged to be standing there. He was my hero.

Rostropovich's grave, Novodevichy Cemetery, Moscow. His widow, Galina Vishnevskaya, stands to the right of the cleric. Photo by the author.

Censorship in the United States
McCarthyism

One of the most notorious periods of American history is the McCarthy era. It began in the very early 1950s when Senator Joseph McCarthy, Republican Senator from Wisconsin, waged a war on communists and communist sympathizers. Many of those McCarthy attacked were neither. One victim was composer Aaron Copland. He was questioned by McCarthy and the House Un-American Activities Committee (HUAC) counsel, Roy Cohn in the spring of 1950:

COHN: Do you feel Communists should be allowed to teach in our schools?

COPLAND: I haven't given the matter much thought as to come up with answer.

COHN: In other words, as of today you don't have any firm thought?

COPLAND: I would be inclined to allow the faculty of the University to decide that.

McCARTHY: Let's say you are on the faculty and are making a designation, would you feel Communists should be allowed to teach?

COPLAND: I couldn't give you a blanket decision on that without knowing the case.

McCARTHY: Let's say the teacher is a Communist, period. Would you feel that is sufficient to bar that teacher from a job as a teacher?

COPLAND: I certainly think it would be sufficient if he were using his Communist membership to angle his teaching to further the purposes of the Communist Party.

Copland managed to escape Senator McCarthy's claws, but exposure by the HUAC had a strong tendency to taint one's reputation. A concert scheduled in 1953 to celebrate the inauguration of president-elect General Dwight D. Eisenhower had Copland's *Lincoln Portrait* listed on the concert program. Representative Fred Busbey, Republican of Illinois, caught wind of the *Lincoln Portrait* programming and objected because "Copland was a Communist." The *Portrait* was removed from the program, despite objections in the press.

In 2000 the National Symphony Orchestra celebrated the hundredth anniversary of Aaron Copland's birth. Among the works performed was the Lincoln Portrait. The concert was presented on three successive evenings, and each evening there was a different narrator, all from the U.S. Congress. On opening night, it was the Speaker of the House, conservative Illinois Republican Denis Hastert. I sat there with my son, distracted by the irony of the performance, forty-seven years after the composition was stricken from Eisenhower's celebration concert.

The Cradle Will Rock

American Mark Blitzstein (1905–64) is probably best known for his adaptation and translation into English of Kurt Weill's popular *Die Dreigroschenoper* (1928) *(The Threepenny Opera)*. That version opened in 1956 at the Theater de Lys in Greenwich Village and featured Weill's widow, Lotte Lenya. It ran for 2,707 performances.

During the Great Depression, Blitzstein wrote *The Cradle Will Rock* (1937). The opera was part of the Federal Theatre Project and was to be directed by twenty-one year old Orson Welles (the next year he would produce his famous radio drama *The War of the Worlds*). I quote *Wikipedia:*

> The musical is a Brechtian allegory of corruption and corporate greed and includes a panoply of societal figures. Set in "Steeltown, USA," it follows the efforts . . . to unionize

the town's workers and combat wicked, greedy businessman, Mr. Mister, who controls the town's factory, press, church and social organization.

Cradle was scheduled to be produced at the Maxine Elliott Theatre on Manhattan's West 39th Street on June 16, 1937. Four days before previews were to begin, the production and all other productions sponsored by the Federal Theatre Project were delayed until at least July 1. The reason stated was budget cuts and the need to reorganize the Works Progress Administration (WPA). The Federal Theatre Project was part of the WPA and employed as many as fifteen thousand actors and actresses at a weekly salary of $23.86. It was widely held that Congressional pressure was the reason for the "need to reorganize."

Nonetheless, over six hundred ticket holders appeared at the theater on opening night. The Maxine Elliott Theatre was dark and the costumes, scenery and music were secured inside. Orson Welles and Mark Blitzstein rented the Venice Theater on Seventh Avenue at West 58th Street. The grumpy and disappointed "audience" outside the Elliott walked north 1.1 miles to the Venice, where a stripped-down performance was given. Music was supplied by the composer on a rented piano, and the singers took seats and sang their solos and duets without costume or props, rising from their places scattered throughout the audience. While many accepted the reasoning for the lockout, many thought it was because of the musical's pro-union, ante-corporate theme.

McCarthyism affected a large number of people. Among them were musicians and composers Elmer Bernstein, Leonard Bernstein, Hanns Eisler, Lena Horne, Otto Klemperer, Dimitri Mitropoulos, Paul Robeson, Pete Seeger, and Artie Shaw.

Marian Anderson

Marian Anderson (1897–1993) was one of the twentieth century's great singers, but because of her race she was denied access to the world of opera. Her career was limited to concert and recital engagements. In 1939 Anderson's management unsuccessfully tried to present a recital at the Daughters of the American Revolution's Constitution Hall in Washington, D.C. The DAR refused rental. The District of Columbia government, then under the control of the U.S. Congress, refused rental of a white public high school's auditorium. A Marian Anderson Citizens Committee was formed under the leadership of the National Association for the Advancement of Colored People (NAACP). Public pressure began and many members of the DAR resigned from the organization, including First Lady Eleanor Roosevelt. Steered by President Franklin D. Roosevelt, a concert was scheduled for Anderson on April 6, 1939, on the steps of the Lincoln Memorial. The Easter Sunday performance attracted seventy-five thousand attendees and was broadcast nationally.

Marian Anderson would have to wait until the age of sixty-two to appear on an opera stage. She sang the role of Ulrica in Verdi's *Masked Ball* at the Metropolitan Opera, where she was the first African American to sing on its stage. (Nuzum. *A Brief History of Banned Music in the United States*)

Courtesy of the Detroit Symphony Orchestra

I Get Ideas

Censorship in the United States also occurred in popular culture. Movies were often blacklisted by such groups as the Catholic Church's National League of Decency. Founded in 1933, it acted as a lobbyist in Hollywood and published a list of movies that Catholics should not see. Its good intentions motivated the film industry to be careful, but probably motivated some of the faithful to attend the banned films.

In 1939 lyricist Yip Harburg and composer Harold Arlen wrote "Lydia, the Tattooed Lady" for the Marx Brothers' *At the Circus.* Decades later Yip Harburg recorded some of his songs and provided some commentary. For *Lydia* he spoke about the studio's reluctance to include one tattoo, specifically one on Lydia's buttocks. The tattoo was a map of the world. So back to the drawing board, and Harburg came up with the idea of replacing the world map with a map of Germany. Anytime Lydia sat down, she would sit down on Hitler's face. That too did not work, so here is what the studio ended up with for the final verse:

> Lydia, oh Lydia, that encyclo-pidia.
> Oh Lydia The Champ of them all.
> She once swept an Admiral clear off his feet.
> The ships on her hips made his heart skip a beat.
> And now the old boy's in command of the fleet,
> for he went and married Lydia!

For two decades from 1933, *Your Hit Parade* was broadcast on the Nation's airwaves, playing the most popular "hits of the week." My family tuned in weekly and listened, anxious to know the hit of the week. But occasionally the airwaves went dead after the announcement of a song. One was a song made popular by Tony Martin in 1951. "I Get Ideas" made the top seven songs for fifteen continuous weeks and was second for four. That led to a total of about forty-five minutes of dead air. Its lyrics follow:

> When we are dancing
> And you're dangerously near me
> I get ideas, I get ideas.
> I want to hold you
> So much closer than I dare to.
> I want to scold you
> 'Cause I care more than I care to.
> And when you touch me
> And there's fire in every finger
> I get ideas, I get ideas.

And after we have kissed goodnight
And still you linger
I kinda think you get ideas too.

Two other banned songs are worth mentioning: Cole Porter's "Love for Sale" (prostitution) and "I Saw Mommy Kissing Santa Claus" (adultery).

Anecdote VIII

I recently learned that a neighbor received a degree in singing from the music school of the University of Colorado, Boulder. He told me that when he was completing his junior year he was promised a major operatic role in the next year's season. He anxiously returned to campus and learned that he would appear in Menotti's *The Medium* as Toby, a mute servant.

Two Trips to Europe

Colmar, France

In the 1990s I traveled to Europe with the Washington Chorus, performing in northern France, Germany, and Austria. The highlight was singing a mass by Mozart in Vienna's Stephansdom, the very church where Mozart was married, baptized two of his children, and from which he was buried. One overnight was in the French city of Colmar. We arrived early, which provided time for a walk around the city. I saw the entrance to the Unterlinden Museum and entered. I was soon in a room crowded with Renaissance art. As I walked around, I turned a corner and came face to face with a most fantastic painting. Never in my life have I been so completely moved by an art work. I was stuck in my tracks and looked at the painting for a very long time. I had no idea what I was looking at, but soon found its label on a nearby wall. It was the Isenheim Alterpiece (1512–1516), a tryptic painted by Matthias Gruenewald (1470–1528). I already knew about the masterpiece but only as a subject in Paul Hindemith's opera *Mathis der*

Gruenewald's Isenheim Altarpiece, Unterlinden Museum, Colmar, France. Photo by the author.

Maler (Mathis the Painter) (1935). Because Hindemith's music was banned by the Nazis, it was never performed in Germany. It did get performances in Zurich and Amsterdam. Wikipedia's entry for *Mathis* sums it up sadly: "The story, set during the German Peasants' War (1524–25), concerns Matthias's struggle for artistic freedom of expression in the repressive climate of his day, which mirrored Hindemith's own struggle as the Nazis attained power and repressed dissent. The opera's obvious political message did not escape the government's notice." What a thrill it was to put the masterpiece painting, completely unknown to me, together with a piece of music with which I was so familiar.

Leipzig, Germany

Gustav Mahler set to work composing music for five poems of the German Friedrich Rueckert (1788–1866) for his composition *Kindertotenlieder* ("Songs on the Death of Children") (1901–04). Rueckert wrote the poems while grieving over the deaths of his two children from scarlet fever. Mahler's daughter Maria was born just weeks before the composition was completed and died of scarlet fever four years later. On a visit to Leipzig in 2015, I attended a concert of the Leipzig String Quartet. The program concluded with a performance of the *Kindertotenlieder*. The soloist was the Lithuanian mezzo-soprano Viktorija Kaminskaite. The concert was held in an old mansion in a room that sat about eighty. While exiting I came face to face with the soloist. I stopped and congratulated her on her performance and said how sad I was each time I heard it, knowing the circumstances of the deaths of the poet's and composer's children. She responded saying, "Yes, I still find it very difficult to sing, even two years after my own child's death."

Only when I experience do I compose — only when I compose do I experience. —Gustav Mahler

"Ah one, and ah two . . ."

After World War II there was a surge of interest in the accordion. I remember six music studios on Detroit's east side that taught scores of children the secrets of all of those buttons on the left hand of the instrument. Knowledge of the accordion did not seem to matter to the studio proprietors. I taught at two of these studios while in high school. The experience was short lived, but at one I was given a few trumpet students. I did play the tuba but not the trumpet. The studio's trumpet teacher gave me a lesson each week and I passed that knowledge down to my students the following week.

Humor and Satire in Music

Be Prepared

It was a Halloween night in the late-1950s. Tom Lehrer was giving a concert at Detroit's Scottish Rite Auditorium. I already knew the lyrics for "The Old Dope Peddler" and was familiar with many of his other songs. I looked forward to a riotous evening and was not disappointed. Lehrer was a Harvard lecturer in mathematics and theater. Two of his songs relate to classical music. One is the "Wiener Schnitzel Waltz," a take on Johann Strauss and Viennese life. The other comments about Alma Mahler's loves and multiple marriages.

> Alma, tell us!
> All modern women are jealous.
> You should have a statue in bronze
> For bagging Gustav and Walter and Franz.
> While married to Gus, she met Gropius,
> And soon she was swinging with Walter.
> Gus died, and her tear drops were copious.
> She cried all the way to the altar.

Alan Sherman

Alan Sherman became famous for his letter from camp to home, "Hello Muddah, Hello Fadduh." His brilliance as a satirist went way beyond when he and the Boston Pops joined forces at the Tanglewood Music Festival in 1964. He opened with a takeoff of Prokofiev's *Peter and the Wolf*, renamed *Peter and the Commissar* in light of Soviet censorship of artists. My favorite was the album's closer, *The End of a Symphony*. Sherman took the codas of several masterpieces and added commentary about their lengths and repetitions:

> No matter which composer, how hallowed be his name,
> They all have good beginnings, but their endings sound the
> same.

With banging on the kettle drums those copper colored metal
  drums,
between the cymbals crashing the brasses keep rehashing,
the—same—darn—notes.
The end of Schubert's "Seventh" should be drastically diminished,
he spent so long on this one that his "Eighth" one went unfinished.
You think the concerts over and you're half way out the door,
and boy do you feel stupid when they start to play some more.

P.D.Q. Bach, the Forgotten Son of J.S. (a.k.a. Peter Schickele)

P.D.Q. Bach, a fictional child of J.S. Bach and Anna Magdalena Bach, "lived" from 1742 to 1807. Composer Peter Schickele
(1935–) gave birth to P.D.Q and the imaginary son made his international debut at Town Hall in 1965. You don't have to listen
to the music to get a chuckle; reading a title or two will gener-
ate one. The "S" after several of the titles is for "Schickele," the
creator's sequential identification of this imaginary composer.
Here are some titles:

Concerto for Bassoon vs. Orchestra
Diverse Ayres on Sundrie Notions
Fanfare for the Common Cold
*Hansel and Gretel and Ted and Alice (an opera in one
    unnatural act)*
*Oedipus Tex, a dramatic oratorio for soloists, chorus, and
    orchestra*
Missa Hilarious, S. N_2O
Safe Sextet, S. R33–L45–R *(pass it once)* 78
The Sanka Cantata
Serenude for Devious Instruments
Shepherd on the Rocks with a Twist
*The Short-Tempered Clavier, Preludes and Fugues in all the
    Major and Minor Keys Except for the Really Hard Ones,*
    S. Easy as 3.14159265
Pervertimento for Bagpipes, Bicycle and Balloons
The Stoned Guest, a half-act opera, S. 86 proof

Schickele is an accomplished bassoonist. His classical output
numbers more than one hundred compositions. He also contrib-
uted words and music to the 1969 Broadway hit, *Oh! Calcutta!*

Victor Borge

Danish-born Victor Borge (1909–2000) became a fixture at theaters throughout the United States and Europe and a radio and television favorite. Sitting at the piano he would deliver wonderful jokes with words and wordplay and play outlandish pieces of music. One of his famous lines was: "The Steinway Piano Company has asked me to announce that I play a Baldwin." He deserves the epithet "The Clown Prince of Denmark."

$$Jack Benny$$

Jack Benny was perhaps the greatest twentieth-century American vaudevillian. Movies, radio, and television made him nationally famous, and his stage persona always made him a tightwad. But in real life Benny was very generous. He donated his time performing on his violin with symphony orchestras throughout the United States, raising money for their pension funds.

In 1959 I had the opportunity to see Benny perform with the Detroit Symphony Orchestra. I was working as the Wayne State University orchestra's librarian. My boss was its conductor Valter Poole, who was also the associate conductor of the DSO. Poole asked me if I was planning to attend the Jack Benny fund-raiser and I told him that I could not afford a ticket (I was happily working for him for a dollar an hour). Poole reached into his pocket and gave me a ticket for the center orchestra. I would have had to pay a hundred dollars for that seat—ten weeks wages.

High school and college classmate Kenneth Goldsmith, now a distinguished violinist and Professor of Violin at the Shepherd School of Music, Rice University, participated in the Benny concert. I will let him tell his own story:

> The underlying idea behind Jack's show was the principle that *everyone on the stage played the violin better than Jack!* The solo players involved were Jack, Misha Mischakoff, and me. During my first season in the DSO I sat on the last stand of the second violins and at the beginning of my second year I was promoted to last chair in the first violin section. This was the perfect spot for my scene with Jack because I could leave the stage quickly without being observed. After opening remarks and about fifteen minutes of hilarious anecdotes, Jack announced that he would attempt to perform Mendelssohn's Violin Concerto and

that, since he experienced a memory slip in Los Angeles the previous evening, he would, with the permission of the audience, use music.

"Oh, Stagehand!" came the call to the wings of the stage . . . This was my cue to enter carrying a music stand . . . The real stagehands had dressed me in old grey pants, a black T-shirt, and a large grey sweater . . . and I entered carrying the very low stand and placed it in front of Mr. Benny. He looked morosely at the lowered stand, handed me his violin while he attempted to raise the stand, and at that moment I put his Stradivarius violin under my chin and ripped off a very flashy cadenza! As I played, Jack very slowly raised the music stand and glared at me, as only he could! I handed the violin back, turned without a word, and sauntered off the stage as he glared at me all the way to the wings! This brief shtick earned great applause and rave reviews in the papers.

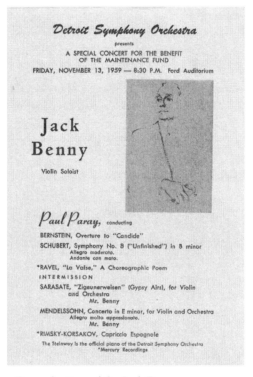

Reproduction of the Jack Benny program.
Used by permission of the Detroit Symphony Orchestra.

Many people in the audience commented that the orchestra musicians found this extremely funny and the reason was that I played a little trick on Mr. Mischakoff, the concertmaster and my teacher. Every violinist has a personal warm-up cadenza and Mischakoff's was especially flashy . . . so I played his warm-up as the showy, virtuoso cadenza and the musicians loved it . . . but Mischakoff did not get it! His assistant concertmaster, Gordon Staples, explained it to him later and Mischa was not amused.

Now enter another violinist, the great Arnold Steinhardt, best known as the first violinist of the Guarneri String Quartet. At age twenty-two Steinhardt was scheduled to perform Mendelssohn's Violin Concerto with the Detroit Symphony Orchestra. The concert was scheduled the evening before the Jack Benny pension fund-raiser.

With Arnold's permission I quote a few paragraphs from his blog, *In the Key of Strawberry.*

I stood in the artist's dressing room, warming up nervously before my sole rehearsal with the Detroit Symphony Orchestra. For a twenty-two-year-old violinist just starting a career, performing Mendelssohn's Violin Concerto with this distinguished group of musicians was an important engagement. My palms were sweating, my heart beat rapidly, and I began to pace back and forth. Grin and bear it, I said to myself. Everything will be all right once you start playing.

There was a knock on the door—undoubtedly the orchestra manager calling me on stage. I sighed with relief. At least the wait was over. I opened the door and stared in disbelief. Standing before me was perhaps the most famous comedian in all of America: Jack Benny. Benny, holding a violin case in his hand, wasted no time. "What's this I hear about you making me look bad, kid?" I opened my mouth to say something but no sound came out. Benny continued unperturbed. "I was supposed to play the Mendelssohn. Now I hear you're doing it. Never mind," he said, brushing past me and placing his violin case next to mine in the dressing room. "I'll do Sarasate's *Gypsy Airs* instead." My pre-concert nerves vanished, replaced by the sensation that I was in the midst of one of those improbable dreams of mine—in this case a private encounter with a man who reached millions of adoring fans on radio and television, a man who, without exaggeration, was an icon of American life and entertainment.

Then the situation took an even more surreal twist. Benny turned to me. "I'm working on a new routine," he said. "This is Mischa Elman trying out a new chin rest. Tell me if you think it's funny." Right, I thought to myself. The great Jack Benny wants my opinion about what's funny—me, a mere fiddle player who forgets a joke's punch line five seconds after it's been told. I shook my head in disbelief. Benny took out his violin and began playing Saint-Saëns's *Introduction and Rondo Capriccioso.* Mischa Elman, one of the reigning violinists, would have been upset to be represented by what I heard. Elman's opulent tone was legendary while Jack Benny's was—how should I put this delicately—awful. Benny readjusted his chin with every little group of notes, never quite getting comfortable and appearing more and more irritated in the process. "Well, what do you think?" Benny asked, looking at me eagerly for approval. I burst out laughing. The skit was indeed very, very funny. Beaming, Benny put his violin back into its case. "Good," he said. "Now let's rehearse with the Detroit Symphony Orchestra." As it turned out, I was to rehearse the Mendelssohn first for a regular subscription concert that night with Benny following immediately afterwards for his slated performance at the orchestra's pension fund concert.

That night, tucked into my Detroit hotel bed, I reviewed the day's events. Foremost on my mind was the Mendelssohn performance. I had played musically, but had there been enough magic? Felix Mendelssohn, the father of this exquisite concerto, would have been disappointed if I, a midwife of sorts, had not delivered his baby successfully. Then I thought of Jack Benny's antics and chuckled in the dark. He had played the violin very badly and made us laugh, a magic of another kind. And finally Mischa Mischakoff's siren sound began playing in my head. Definitely magic.

Danny Kaye

He learned the scores by ear but regularly conducted world-famous orchestras. Kaye's style, even if accompanied by unpredictable antics (he once traded the baton for a fly swatter to conduct

The Flight of the Bumblebee) was praised by the likes of Zubin Mehta and Dimitri Mitropoulos. Over his career Kaye raised over five million dollars for musician pension funds.

> *Wagner's music is not as bad as it sounds.* —Mark Twain

Dry at Low Heat

In London there is a musical group called Unexpected Opera which performs *The Rinse Cycle,* a two-hour version of Wagner's sixteen hour, four-opera *Ring* cycle with a cast of five.

Illustration by Kim Borrego

Things That Do Not Fit Anywhere Else

Two flutes meet while walking down a street. One says to the other, "Who was that piccolo that I saw you out with last evening?" The second flute replies, "That wasn't a piccolo, that was my fife."

A one sentence review: "The music was so bad it didn't even get a standing ovation."

Bumper sticker: "I am pro-accordion and I vote!"

Q. What do drummers [or your choice] use for contraception?
A. Their personalities.

On March 6, 1960, the pianist Francis Poulenc and singer Denise Duval gave a recital of Poulenc's works in Detroit. I was working at radio station WDET-FM and arranged to interview the great French artist. That morning he came to our studio and after a brief conversation Poulenc began perusing the extensive library of LPs that lined two walls of the office. The very last recording on a shelf was his *Babar the Elephant.* Poulenc bent over and retrieved the record, examined the front and back covers and turned to me and said, "Junk!" We proceeded to the studio where an engineer awaited. The tape started rolling and I read my introduction and asked the first question. Poulenc turned and asked if I spoke French. I replied no, and he stood up, said "no interview" and walked out of the studio. I regret that I did not save the tape of that short encounter, but I was too disappointed to think.

The following is a caption of a photograph published in the Chicago-Sun Times: "Dr. Arthur Rubinstein, Larry Pogofsky, Dr. Joseph Dirsner and Denise Rubinstein joined more than 600 guests at the Hyatt Regency Chicago, who enjoyed music tied to the party's theme: 'Gastro-Intestinal Research Foundation Salutes American Music.'"

mu·sic agent n. (myoozic ājənt) One who reluctantly gives up ninety percent of his salary to the artist he or she represents.

A traffic sign in Havana, Cuba. Photo by the author.

Many of the less successful leaders of the 1940s big bands were not musicians. They were businessmen who stood in front of the band, introduced songs and soloists, and waved (sometimes convincingly) a baton. One of these leaders was known to regularly rehearse his group and it was hell for the musicians. At one particularly bad session and after a long rant by the leader, he turned and walked away from the band. Immediately the drummer played a snare drum riff, much like one would hear after a comedian's bad joke. The leader made a quick about face and yelled, "Who did that?"

Drummers are people who hang out with musicians.

Q. When you hear a knock at the door, how can you tell it's a soprano?

A. She doesn't know when to come in.

The world-famous cellist Yo-Yo Ma and United Nations leader Boutros Boutros-Ghali once dined together in New York. Ma had a dish of Po Po Chicken and Boutros-Ghali had Mahi-Mahi. Half way through the meal their waiter came by and asked, "How are your meals?" Without hesitation and in unison, they both replied "So, so"!

Ralph Sharon, singer Tony Bennet's pianist for more than four decades, performed weekly at a Boulder, Colorado restaurant in his retirement, and I had the good fortune of visiting with him on several occasions. At one of those meetings he told the following story:

So, three notes walk into a bar—a C, G, and an E-flat. The bartender looks up and says, "we do not serve minors." So the E-flat leaves and the other two share a fifth between them. After a few drinks the G is out flat and its experience diminished. Eventually the C sobers up, finds one of his friends missing and the other passed out. C realizes to his horror that he's under a rest. C is brought to trial, found guilty and convicted to ten years of D.S. without Coda at the Paul Williams/Neil Sedaka Correctional Facility.

A friend, who prefers that I not use her name, provided the following story. Let's call her by her initials—KDB. KDB possesses a beautiful soprano voice (and I add a matching physical beauty). Educated in the Southwest, she went to New York City to seek her fame. After a year of working as a singing waitress and auditioning frequently, she got a job in a chorus of a now defunct opera company. In mid-season the company performed Richard Strauss's *Salome*. On opening night and just before Salome was to begin her "Dance of the Seven Veils" the lead dramatic soprano slipped and twisted her ankle. From the wings came a shout "KDB, step in and do the dance." So KBD, shy as she is, did — without the veils and with the full realization of the audience. Near the end of the number someone in the audience shouted, "Shake it babe!" After retirement from the chorus KDB decided to go back to the other part of her double college major — percussion. She landed a position in a semi-professional community orchestra. Her first gig was performing Liszt's Piano Concerto No. 1, often referred to as "The Triangle Concerto." How ironic, she said. The triangle was always my favorite.

"A true music lover is one who on hearing a blonde soprano singing in the bathtub puts his ear to the keyhole. "
— Anonymous, from Slonimsky's *A Thing or Two about Music*

During my retirement I seasonally worked as a tax preparer and one year attended a conference of the National Association of Tax Professionals in Reno, Nevada. The keynote speaker was a regional commissioner of the Internal Revenue Service. He opened his remarks with a story about how difficult it was for him to attend social events. Once people found out about his employer, they tended to ignore him. He then quoted his favorite bumper sticker: "Please don't tell mama I work for the IRS. She thinks I play piano in a whorehouse."

"I can hold a note as long as the Chase National Bank."
— Ethel Merman

Noah Greenberg (1919–1966) founded the New York Pro Musica in 1952. During his fourteen years of directing the ensemble, more than twenty-five LP recordings were issued, igniting a national interest in Medieval and Renaissance music. He also edited the music for *An Elizabethan Song Book* which includes *Tobacco Is Like Love* by the Scottish composer Tobias Hume (c. 1579–1645). I quote some of the lyrics:

Love maketh leane the fatte mens tumor, so doth Tobacco,
Love still dries uppe the wanton humor, so doth Tobacco,

Love makes men sayle from shore to shore, so doth Tobacco
Tis fond love often makes men poor, so doth Tobacco
Love makes men scorn al Coward feares, so doth Tobacco
Love often sets men by the eares, so doth Tobacco.

Frank Gill, music critic for the *Detroit Times* during the 1950s, told me that the most colorful music writers came from the sports desk. After reading reviews for six decades, I can believe that. Lots of color but not much content. In his fine book *Musical Blunders*, Fritz Spiegl tells of a critic who left a concert early and wrote a review saying that nothing eventful happened at the concert. Well, nothing but that "a deranged person had leapt from the balcony into the hall and attacked the conductor . . ."

Violinist Zachery Carrettin and pianist Mina Gajic moved to Boulder, Colorado in 2014. Zach had been named director of the Boulder Bach Festival and Mina the director of its education outreach program. Concurrent to their move was an 1895-period piano coming from the Netherlands. Its shipping date did not coincide with their arrival in Boulder. Mina did not have an instrument for practice, so I opened my home to her and she began making visits to play my Steinway. Two hours after her very first visit, I met a neighbor who said, "Boy, Arthur, your piano playing sure sounded good today." "Thanks," I replied and hurried away.

In 1956 the German Democratic Republic issued a commemorative stamp for the centennial of the death of composer Robert Schumann. The portrait of the composer was beautifully engraved, but the background music score was a blatant error. It was the music of Franz Schubert. Thousands of the stamps were sold before it was corrected and reissued.

I am saddened by the absence of music education in our schools. Our country is denying its students learning about this great art. "Air Guitar" competitions will never take its place. When I reflect on my music education in 1950s Detroit, I am amazed and appreciative of the quality. In the eighth and ninth grades I attended school six days a week. On Saturday mornings I played string bass in the All-City Orchestra and in the afternoons played tuba in the All-City Band. In high school my classmates included Isidor Saslav and Dorothy Pixley Rothchild. "Izzy" later served as concertmaster of the Baltimore, Buffalo, Minneapolis, and New Zealand orchestras. Dorothy became Leopold Stokowski's first concertmistress of the American Symphony Orchestra. She also taught at Julliard. In high school she performed the Mendelssohn Violin Concerto with our orchestra and a few weeks later played a Mendelssohn Piano Concerto with the Detroit Symphony Orchestra. Cellist Robert Newkirk became principal of the Kennedy Opera House Orchestra. Donald Sinta is now regarded as the greatest alto saxophone player in the world. Ron Carter played with Miles Davis in his early years and is now the most recorded jazz bassist ever. Shirley Love, Muriel Costa-Greenspon, and Delores Ivory Davis enjoyed decades-long careers with the Metropolitan Opera, the New York City Opera, and the Houston Opera companies respectively. Violinist David Cerone led the Cleveland Institute of Music from 1985 to 2008. Kenneth Goldsmith is a distinguished violin teacher at Rice University. Bruce Galbraith became Director of the Arts Academy/Vice President of Interlochen for eight years. And Mary Jane Tomlin (a.k.a. Lily Tomlin) was our cheerleader. All of this in the three years that I attended the Cass Technical High School, a "magnet school" before that phrase came into use. How lucky we were to have a great music curriculum.

My high school classmate, Muriel Costa-Greenspon, in costume for a 1981 performance of *Carmen* with the New York City Opera. Wolf Trap National Park for the Performing Arts. Vienna, Virginia. Photo by the author.

A Liszt [sic] of the Full Names of Great Composers

Samuel Osborne Barber II
Béla Viktor János Bartók
Alban Maria Johannes Berg
Alexandre César Léopold Bizet
Edward Benjamin Britten

Alexis Emmanuel Chabrier
Carlos Antonio de Padua Chávez y Ramírez
Frédéric François Chopin
George Michael Cohan
Edward Elzear "Zez" Confrey

Chopin's grave, Le Cimetière du Père-Lachaise, Paris.
Photo by the author.

Claude-Achille Debussy
Domenico Gaetano Maria Donizetti
Antonín Leopold Dvořák
Edward Kennedy "Duke" Ellington

Manuel de Falla y Matheu
Gabriel Urbain Fauré
César-Auguste-Jean-Guillaume-Hubert Franck

George Jacob Gershwin
Alberto Evaristo Ginastera
Percy Aldridge Grainger
Edvard Hagerup Grieg

Jacques François Antoine Marie Ibert

Edward Alexander MacDowell
Alma Maria Mahler Gropius Werfel, nee Schindler
Pietro Antonio Stefano Mascagni
Jules Émile Frédéric Massenet
Jakob Ludwig Felix Mendelssohn Bartholdy
Claudio Giovanni Antonio Monteverdi
Johann Georg Leopold Mozart
Johannes Chrysostomus Wolfgangus Theophilus Mozart (The
    introduction of "Amadeus" into his name dates to a signed
    letter in a mocking Latin, Wolfgangus Amadeus Mozartus.
    In Latin, Amadeus means "God's love.")
Modest Petrovich Mussorgsky

Carl August Nielsen

Giacomo Antonio Domenico Michele Secondo Maria Puccini

Vito Tongiani's bronze monument to Giacomo Puccini stands outside the composer's birthplace, Lucca, Italy. Photo by the author.

Joseph Maurice Ravel
Gioachino Antonio Rossini

Éric Alfred Leslie Satie
Franz Peter Schubert

Giuseppe Fortunino Francesco Verdi (a.k.a. Joe Green)
Antonio Lucio Vivaldi

Wilhelm Richard Wagner
Carl Maria Friedrich Ernst von Weber

What's in a Name?

And now a word from our . . .

Announcer: "And now we will hear a work by Rimsky and his brother Korsakoff."

And up next . . .

Announcer: "And here is that great American song, 'Strike Up the Band,' by George Gershwin and his sister, Ira."

Transliterations

Dictionary.com defines "transliteration" as "to change (letters, words, etc.) into corresponding characters of another alphabet or language." A name with which we are most familiar, Петр Ильич Чайковский, has given writers, editors, librarians, and publishers a great amount of trouble and anguish. In English we know that name to be Peter Ilyich Tchaikovsky. But according to writer Brett Langston, Tchaikovsky himself used three different transliterations in his writing: Tchaikovsky, Tschaikowsky, and Tchaikovsky.

When I joined the staff of the Library of Congress in 1964, the head of music cataloging was editing the music card catalog, attempting to bring all of the works of and about Tchaikovsky under one spelling, a task that was interrupted by her retirement.

Here is a Liszt [sic] of other transliterations of that Russian composer's name:

- Tschaikowsky, Peter Iljitch
- Ciaikovsky, Piotr Ilic
- Tchaikowsky, Peter Iljitch
- Ciaikovsky, Pjotr Iljc
- Cajkovskij, Petr Il'ic
- Tsjaikovsky, Peter Iljitsj
- Czajkowski, Piotr
- Chaikovsky, P. I.
- Csajkovszkij, Pjotr Iljics
- Tsjaïkovskiej, Pjotr Iljietsj

- Tjajkovskij, Pjotr Ilitj
- Čaikovskis, P.
- Chaĭkovskiĭ, Petr Il'ich
- Tchaikovski, Piotr
- Tchaikovski, Piotr Ilyitch,
- Chaĭkovskiĭ, Petr
- Tchaikovsky, Peter
- Tchaïkovsky, Piotr Ilitch
- Tschaikowsky, Pjotr Iljitsch
- Tchaikowsky, Pyotr
- Tschajkowskij, Pjotr Iljitsch
- Tchaïkovski, P. I.
- Ciaikovskij, Piotr
- Ciaikovskji, Piotr Ilijich
- Tschaikowski, Peter Illic
- Tjajkovskij, Peter
- Chaĭkovski, P'otr Ilich,
- Tschaikousky, P.I.
- Tschaijkowskij, P. I.
- Chaĭkovski, Piotr Ilich
- Tchaikovsky, Pyotr Ilyich
- Čajkovskij, Pëtr Ilič
- Tchaikovsky, Peter Ilyich
- Tchaikofsky, Peter Ilyitch
- Tciaikowski, P.
- Tchaïkovski, Petr Ilitch
- Ciaikovski, Peter Ilic
- Tschaikowski, Pjotr
- Tchaikovskij, Piotr Ilic

A.K.A.

Shostakovich = Chocolakovich

Weill/Gershwin, i.e., Ira

After his brother's death, Ira Gershwin worked with other composers, and one successful partnership was with Kurt Weill. The collaboration created the 1941 musical *Lady in the Dark* and featured an unknown Broadway face by the name of Danny Kaye. Kaye stole the show with his performance of "Tschaikowsky (and

Other Russians)." Reminiscent of a Gilbert and Sullivan patter song, Kaye raced through, a cappella, the names of fifty Russian composers. Well, not quite. Three were names of Polish composers and one was American Vernon Duke, whose birth name was Vladimir Aleksandrovich Dukelsky. To make the lyrics work, Gershwin took poetic liberties with many of the spellings.

Wikipedia lists the names used in the song with their correct spelling and the order in which they are sung: Witold Maliszewski, Anton Rubinstein, Anton Arensky, Pyotr Ilyich Tchaikovsky, Wassily Sapellnikoff, Nikolay Dmitriev, Alexander Tcherepnin, Ivan Kryzhanovsky, Leopold Godowsky, Nikolai Artsybushev, Stanisław Moniuszko, Fyodor Akimenko, Nicolai Soloviev, Sergei Prokofiev, Dimitri Tiomkin, Arseny Koreshchenko, Mikhail Glinka, Alexander Winkler, Dmitry Bortniansky, Vladimir Rebikov, Alexander Ilyinsky, Nikolai Medtner, Mily Balakirev, Vasily Zolotaryov, Alexander Kvoschinsky, Nikolay Sokolov, Alexander Kopylov, Vernon Duke (born Dukelsky), Nikolay Klenovsky, Dmitri Shostakovich, Alexander Borodin, Reinhold Glière, David Nowakowsky, Anatoly Lyadov, Genari Karganoff, Igor Markevitch, Pantschenko, Alexander Dargomyzhsky, Vladimir Shcherbachov, Alexander Scriabin, Sergei Vasilenko, Igor Stravinsky, Nikolai Rimsky-Korsakov, Modest Mussorgsky, Alexander Gretchaninov, Alexander Glazunov, César Cui, Vasily Kalinnikov, Sergei Rachmaninoff, and Joseph Rumshinsky.

Give a listen on YouTube. (https://www.youtube.com/watch?v=PkJdmTrlTYk).

Deaths of Musicians

What a Way to Go

Jane Little was a contrabassist with the Atlanta Symphony Orchestra from 1945 to her death in 2016. Seventy-one seasons—a very secure record in the *Guinness Book of World Records*. Her career began when it was rare to have females in symphony orchestras, harpists being the exception. Jane Little lived up to her name. She stood at four feet, eleven inches, a handicap considering the size of a string bass. On May 15, 2016, while playing Irving Berlin's "There's No Business Like Show Business," she collapsed and died on stage during a pops concert.

Neither of Schoenberg's Famous Students Faired Well

Alban Berg was bitten by an insect which produced a boil on his back. His wife used scissors to treat it, and the procedure resulted in blood poisoning.

Anton von Webern was a casualty of World War II. In the city of Mittersill, Austria, he was visiting the home of his son-in-law. He went outside to smoke a cigarette and was shot. He did not know that the property was surrounded by the military. He was killed by an American soldier.

Oh, You Naughty Boys

Composer Alessandro Stradella was stabbed to death in 1682 in Genoa, Italy. The hired killer was never identified, but it is believed that a nobleman of the Lomellini Family hired the assassin to put an end to the victim's infidelities.

British composer Henry Purcell died on November 21, 1695. One theory of his death is that he caught a chill and things proceeded from there. Why the chill? He returned home late from the theater and his wife locked him out! Why? Franklin Zimmerman alleges in his biography that Mrs. Purcell "so disapproved of her husband's habitual carousing."

Medical Problems

Alexander Scriabin developed a furuncle on his upper lip, the same location where another had once occurred. Alfred Swan's biography of Scriabin reports that in just a few days a fever developed, and in spite of intensive medical care and attention, the infection eventually covered his entire face. Then pleurisy set in, and he died on April 14, 1915.

Jean-Baptiste Lully (1632–1687) was conducting a performance of his *Te Deum* using a conductor's staff. It was common practice in the seventeenth century for conductors to use a long staff, raising it up and down to indicate the rhythm. During the performance he smashed his toe, and it became infected. He refused amputation because it would prohibit him from dancing. Gangrene set in, and he died in Paris.

Death by Transport

The Belgium composer Ceasar Frank died as a result of an accident when a horse-drawn trolley struck the cab in which he was riding.

Ernest Chausson was forty-four years old when he rode a bicycle downhill and struck a wall. He died instantly on June 10, 1899.

He Should Have Waited a Few Days

Sergei Prokofiev died of suffocation on March 5, 1953. His death went virtually unnoticed because fifty minutes later Joseph Stalin, general secretary of the Communist Party's Central Committee, passed. It took three days before Prokofiev's death was announced to the world.

Is the Printed Program Always Correct?

This is a story told to Bruce Galbraith, retired Interlochen vice-president and director of the Interlochen Arts Academy.

Roger E. Jacobi began his Interlochen work while still on the faculty of the University of Michigan. In the summers, Roger and his equally talented wife, Mary Jane, would work in northern Michigan at the (then called) National Music Camp. Roger, a notorious stickler for details and accuracy served as Program Director and one of his responsibilities was to print each and every concert program. He didn't like to make misteaks [sic].

This most memorable event took place in the days of the mimeograph machine, a device that required typing all information onto a purple ditto master, correcting any noticed errors with a small brush of odorous correcting fluid. The process was very time-consuming. Just as the programs were being handed out one warm July evening in 1956, it was noticed that the fourth movement of the programed Brahms quartet had not been listed on the program. Too late to laboriously change anything, the faculty string quartet proceeded with their performance in the legendary Kresge Auditorium. Just after the third movement had concluded, the second violinist, Ottokar Cadek, handed his violin to the first violinist, collapsed and died. The fourth movement was not listed in the program, nor was it ever played. Ever since that time, rumors about Cadek's ghost on the Kresge stage have circulated. Some say it's directed at stage crew members, reminding them to slow down and take it easy. It is said that often when things are scurrying toward an upcoming performance the lights flicker as a warning. Likewise, many Interlochen faculty members have often picked up a soon-to-be distributed program to confirm that their name is listed!

Your music—dear me, it is a sort of luggage van to the kingdom of heaven. —Franz von Lenbach to Richard Wagner

The Paris graves of Edith Piaf (Cimetière du Père Lachaised), Hector Berlioz (Cimetière de Montmartre) and Tchaikovsky's grave marker (St. Petersburg's Tikhvinskoye Cemetery). Photos by the author.

If Food be the Nourishment of Music, Eat on!

Music with dinner is an insult both to the cook and violinist.
—G. K. Chesterton, *Watson's Dictionary of Musical Quotations*

There are several food preparations that are attributed to or named after composers. The Australian soprano Nellie Melba provides the name for peach melba and melba toast. Tournedos Rossini is named after the opera composer and contains pan fried beef with foie gras. The great Italian tenor Enrico Caruso gives his name to Uruguayan Caruso sauce made of cream, onions, cheese, ham, nuts, and mushrooms. And Hector Berlioz is remembered by eggs Berlioz, a combination of soft-boiled eggs, potatoes, mushrooms, and truffles. In Portland, Oregon, there is a café called "The Rimsky-Korsakoffe House."

A Thanksgiving greeting created by Kim Borrego and given to me on my favorite holiday. I never realized that turkeys played the accordion.

Trivia IX

Trunk songs are songs that composers wrote for a particular Broadway show or movie but removed during production. The music and lyrics were placed in a trunk for possible future use, with or without the original words. The most famous trunk song is "Blue Moon" by Richard Rogers and Lorenz Hart. It was first written for the MGM movie *Hollywood Party* with the title "Prayer." The movie never made the silver screen nor was the song recorded. In its second resurrection Lorenz Hart wrote new lyrics for the film *Manhattan Melodrama,* and the melody with the title "It's Just That Kind of Play" was given new life. It was eventually cut from the film. Another failed version (the third), "The Bad in Ev'ry Man," was also thrown into the trunk. Finally "Blue Moon" emerged, and we've known it ever since with the wonderful opening Lorenz Hart lyric's: "Blue moon/you saw me standing alone/without a dream in my heart/without a love of my own." "Blue Moon" never did reach Broadway show or motion picture status.

One of the most recognized American songs is Irving Berlin's "Easter Parade" (1933). Its words also had a bad start under the title "Smile and Show Your Dimple" (1917).

We are not an aria country. We are a song country.
—Alan Jay Lerner

Words on Music

"Music is the movement of sound to reach the soul for the education of its virtue." Plato.

"Music is the art of the prophets and the gift of God." Martin Luther.

"Music is the shorthand of emotion." Leo Tolstoy.

On understanding and appreciating modern music: "Youth has an advantage; they have less to unlearn." James Bailey, former music curator, Dairy Arts Center, Boulder, Colorado. Cellist and jazz saxophonist.

"Composing gives me great pleasure . . . there is nothing that surpasses the joy of creation, if only because through it one wins hours of self-forgetfulness, when one lives in a world of sound." Clara Schumann.

"Composers shouldn't think too much—it interferes with their plagiarism." American song lyricist Howard Dietz.

"So far as genius can exist in a man who is merely virtuous, Haydn had it. He went as far as the limits that morality sets to the intellect." Friedrich Nietzsche.

"There's nothing remarkable about it. All one has to do is hit the right keys at the right time and the instrument plays itself." Johann Sebastian Bach.

"I have played over the music of that scoundrel Brahms. What a giftless bastard! It annoys me that this self-inflated mediocrity is hailed as a genius. Why, in comparison with him, Raff is a giant, not to speak of Rubenstein, who after all is a live and important human being, while Brahms is chaotic and absolutely dried-up stuff." Pyotr Ilyich Tchaikovsky.

"Too many pieces of music finish too long after the end." Igor Stravinsky.

"Writing about music is like dancing about architecture." Thelonious Monk.

"Jazz is the folk music of the machine age." Paul Whiteman.

"Life is a lot like jazz—it's best when you improvise." George Gershwin.

"Jazz is the music of the body. The breath comes through brass. It is the body's breath, and the strings' wails and moans are echoes of the body's music. It is the body's vibrations which ripple from the fingers. And the mystery of the withheld theme, known to jazz musicians alone, is like the mystery of our secret life. We give to others only peripheral improvisations." Anaïs Nin.

"Without music, life would be a mistake." Friedrich Nietzsche.

"I think I should have no other mortal wants if I could always have plenty of music. It seems to infuse strength into my limbs and ideas into my brain. Life seems to go on without effort when I am filled with music." George Bernard Shaw.

Appendix A

Answers to Quizzes I, II, and III

Question 1: Which American composer was born on the Fourth of July? The answer is Steven Foster. Copland was born on November 14; Bernstein on August 25; Cohen on July 3; and McDowell on December 18. Calvin Coolidge was the only American president to be born on the Fourth of July. Other American notables who share that birthdate are artist Rube Goldberg, musician Mitch Miller, playwright Neil Simon, and Esther Pauline "Eppie" Lederer, a.k.a. advice columnist Ann Landers. Whoops! I forgot one—Roy Rogers' horse Trigger.

Question 2: Who did not write five piano concerti? Frédéric François Chopin. Chopin wrote only two concertos for piano and orchestra. Prokofiev began a sixth piano concerto but died before it was completed.

Question 3: Who wrote the text for "Ode to Joy" that is used in the final movement of Beethoven's "Choral" Symphony? Friedrich von Schiller wrote the poem in 1785 and revised it in 1803. Beethoven used the latter, but only parts of it and not in the exact order. In 1985 it became the anthem of the European Union.

Question 4: What is the oldest U.S. symphony orchestra? The New York Philharmonic. It began its distinguished life in 1842 under the name Philharmonic Society. Next was the St. Louis Symphony, founded in 1880. The Boston and Chicago Symphony Orchestras were founded in 1881 and 1891 respectively. It would not be until the beginning of the Great Depression that Washington, D.C.'s National Symphony Orchestra would begin performances in 1931.

Question 5: Which composer lived the shortest life? Lili Boulanger, the sister of Nadia Boulanger, lived for only twenty-four years. Her creative output is modest but well documented on recordings. She was a student of Fauré and the first woman ever to win the Prix de Rome. Franz Schubert's life was cut short at age thirty-one. Mozart lived for thirty-five years, and George Bizet lived one year longer. Gershwin lived for thirty-eight years.

Question 6: Which composer lived the longest life? The little-known Russian American avant-garde composer Leon Ornstein lived for 108 years (1892–2002). American Elliott Carter lived for 103 (1908–2012). His *Instances for Chamber Orchestra, Dialogues II for Piano and Chamber Orchestra,* and *Epigrams for Violin, Cello, and Orchestra* were all completed during his final year of life. Irving Berlin and Nicholas Slonimsky were both centenarians plus one. The French modernist Henri Dutilleux lived for 97 years.

Question 7: Who was not a member of the "The Mighty Handful?" Tchaikovsky. "The Mighty Handful", a.k.a. "The Mighty Five," "The New Russian School," and "Могучая кучка," dominated Russian nationalist music during the mid-nineteenth century. Led by Mily Balakirev the group consisted of composers Alexander Borodin, Modeste Mussorgsky, and Nicolai Rimsky-Korsakov. They were later joined by César Cui. It is interesting that these composers had other occupations. Borodin was a chemist, Mussorgsky worked for the government's forest department, Rimsky-Korsakov was an officer in the Imperial Russian Navy, Cui was a military engineer, and depending on what you read, Balakirev was independently wealthy (Slonimsky's *A Thing or Two About Music*) or came from a "poor clerk's family" (*Wikipedia*).

Much further south and seventy-five years later the phrase "Les Six" was penned. It referred to Georges Auric (1899–1983), Louis Durey (1888–1979), Arthur Honegger (1892–1955), Darius Milhaud (1892–1974), Francis Poulenc (1899–1963), and Germaine Tailleferre (1892–1983), all young French composers (except the Swiss-born Honegger) rebelling against the dominating musical influences of Richard Wagner, Claude Debussy, and Maurice Ravel in early-twentieth-century France.

Question 8: Which of the following musicals had the longest run in America? *The Fantastics,* with music by Harvey Schmidt and lyrics by Tom Jones. The show opened in 1960 in the Off-Broadway Sullivan Street Playhouse. Its original run went on for forty-two years—17,162 performances! Andrew Lloyd Weber's *Phantom of the Opera* is next with over 12,000 performances. *The Lion King* and *Chorus Line* come in third and fourth.

Oklahoma! opened in 1943 and closed after 2,212 performances—a record for its time. On July 12, 1995, I was in New York City and attended a celebration of Oscar Hammerstein's one hundredth birthday. It was held on a set for *Show Boat* that was running at one of Broadway's theaters. There were songs and tributes, but what I remember best was the presentation by the director of the Oscar Hammerstein Foundation. He told the audience that there was not a single minute in the preceding fifty-two weeks that *Oklahoma!* was not being performed somewhere in the world. Now that is a theatrical record!

Question 9: Which composer did Ira Gershwin not write lyrics for? Cole Porter. Porter, like Irving Berlin, wrote his own lyrics. In 1934 Ira teamed with Harold Arlen for *Life Begins at 8:40*. In 1944 he worked with Jerome Kern on the movie *Cover Girl*, and in 1950 he was lyricist for Weill's *Lady in the Dark.*

Recommended Reading

5000 Nights at the Opera by Rudolf Bing. Garden City, NY: Doubleday, 1972.

Bad Boy of Music by George Antheil. Hollywood: Samuel French, 1990.

Beethoven's Hair by Russell Martin. New York: Russell Martin, 2001.

Diaghilev's Ballets Russes by Lynn Carafola. New York: Oxford University Press, 1989.

Fritz Spiegl's Book of Musical Blunders and Other Musical Curiosities. London: Robson, 1996.

Galina: A Russian Story by Galina Vishnevskaya. San Diego: Harcourt, Brace, Jovanovich, 1984.

Lectionary of Music by Nicolas Slonimsky. New York: Anchor, 1990.

Lexicon of Musical Invective: Critical Assaults on Composers since Beethoven's Time by Nicolas Slonimsky. Seattle: University of Washington Press, 1965.

Lives, Wives, and Loves of the Great Composers by Fritz Spiegl. London: Boyars, 1997.

The Lyric Opera Companion: the History, Lore, and Stories of the World's Greatest Operas. Kansas City: Andrews and McMeel, 1991.

Lyrics on Several Occasions by Ira Gershwin. New York: Knopf, n.d.

Memoirs of an Amnesiac by Oscar Levant. New York: Bantam, 1965.

Musicophilia: Tales of Music and the Brain by Oliver Sacks. New York. Knopf, 2007.

The Ox on the Roof: Scenes of Musical Life in Paris in the Twenties by Games Harding. London: McDonald, 1972.

Paris: the Musical Kaleidoscope, 1870-1925 by Elaine Brody. New York, George Braziller, 1987.

Perfect Pitch by Nicolas Slonimsky. New York: Oxford University Press, 1988.

Polkas and Pierogies, by Arthur J. Lieb. Boulder: Squeeze Box Press, 2015.

The Piano Shop on the Left Bank: Discovering a Forgotten Passion in a Paris Atelier by Thaddeus Carhart. New York: Random House Trade Paperbacks, 2002.

The Study of Ethnomusicology: Thirty-Three Discussions by Bruno Nettl. Urbana: University of Illinois Press, 2015.

They Told Me Not to Take That Job: Tumult, Betrayal, Heroics, and the Transformation of Lincoln Center by Richard Levy. New York: *Public Affairs*, 2015.

A Thing or Two about Music by Nicolas Slonimsky. New York: Allen, Towne & Heath, 1948.

What to Listen for in Music by Aaron Copland. New York: Signet Classics, 2011.

The Wordsworth Dictionary of Musical Quotations by Derek Watson. Edinburgh: Wordsworth Reference, 1994.

Selected Bibliography

Apel, Willi. *Harvard Dictionary of Music*. Cambridge: Harvard University Press, 1961.

Bach, Johann Sebastian. *Werke*. Ann Arbor: J.W. Edwards, 1947.

Barlow, Michael. *Whom the Gods Love: The Life and Music of George Butterworth*. London: Toccata, 1997.

Bowers, Faubion. *Scriabin: A Biography*. New York: Dover, 1996.

Brandt, Nat. *Con Brio: Four Russians Called the Budapest String Quartet*. New York: Oxford University Press, 1993.

Chailley, Jacques. *40,000 Years of Music; Man in Search of Music*. New York: Farrar, Straus & Giroux, 1964.

Cohen, Harvey G. *Duke Ellington's America*. Chicago: University of Chicago Press, 2010.

Collier, James Lincoln. *Duke Ellington*. New York: Oxford University Press, 1987.

"Famous Quotes at BrainyQuote." BrainyQuote, http://www.brainyquote.com.

Gianturco, Carolyn. *Alessandro Stradella, 1639–1682: His Life and Music*. Oxford: Clarendon, 1994.

"Goodreads." Goodreads, http://www.goodreads.com.

Gordon, Eric A. *Mark the Music: The Life and Work of Marc Blitzstein*. New York: St. Martin's, 1989.

Gordon, Robert. *The Oxford Handbook of Sondheim Studies*. Oxford: Oxford University Press, 2014.

Grove, George, and Stanley Sadie. *The New Grove Dictionary of Music and Musicians*. London: Macmillan, 2001.

Handbook of Musical Statistics. Boston: Boston Musical Bureau, 1902.

Hayes, Malcolm. *Anton Von Webern*. London: Phaidon, 1995.

Hodeir, André. *Jazz: Its Evolution and Essence*. New York: Grove, 1956.

Hume, Paul. "Margaret Truman Sings Here Again with Light Program." *Washington Post*, December 6, 1950.

Jelagin, Juri. *Taming of the Arts*. New York: Dutton, 1951.

Joseph, Charles M. *Stravinsky & Balanchine: A Journey of Invention*. New Haven: Yale University Press, 2002.

Kavanaugh, Patrick. *Music of the Great Composers: A Listener's Guide to the Best of Classical Music*. Grand Rapids: Zondervan Publishing House, 1996.

Kernfeld, Barry Dean. *The New Grove Dictionary of Jazz*. New York: St. Martin's Press, 1994.

Kolneder, Walter. *Anton Webern, an Introduction to His Works.* London: Faber and Faber, 1968.

Latham, Alison. *The Oxford Companion to Music.* Oxford: Oxford University Press, 2002.

Lichtenwanger, William. *The Music of the Star-spangled Banner.* Washington: Library of Congress, 1977.

Mallaby, Sebastian. *The Man Who Knew: The Life and times of Alan Greenspan.* New York: Penguin, 2016.

Merriam-Webster's Collegiate Dictionary. Springfield: Merriam-Webster, 2003.

Marrocco, W. Thomas. "The String Quartet Attributed to Benjamin Franklin." *Proceedings of the American Philosophical Society* 116, no. 6 (1972): 477-85.

Mozart, Wolfgang Amadeus. *Wolfgang Amadeus Mozart Is a Dirty Old Man the Scatolological Canons and Songs.* Epic, 1967, 33⅓ rpm.

"Music Resources on Classical Music, Opera, Jazz, Rock, Learning Music, and More." The website of *Music With Ease,* http://www.musicwithease.com.

Nin, Anaïs, and Gunther Stuhlmann. *The Diary of Anaïs Nin.* San Diego: Harcourt Brace Jovanovich, 1975.

Nuzum, Eric. *Parental Advisory: Music Censorship in America.* New York: Perennial, 2001.

Peress, Maurice. *Dvořák to Duke Ellington: A Conductor Explores America's Music and Its African American Roots.* Oxford: Oxford University Press, 2004.

Pollack, Howard. *Aaron Copland: The Life and Work of an Uncommon Man.* New York: Henry Holt, 1999.

Prokofiev, Sergey. *Prokofiev by Prokofiev: A Composer's Memoir.* Garden City: Doubleday, 1979.

Robinson, Harlow. *Sergei Prokofiev: A Biography.* 1st Paperback Edition. New York: Viking, 1988.

Ross, Alex. *The Rest Is Noise: Listening to the Twentieth Century.* New York: Farrar, Straus and Giroux, 2007.

Sacks, Oliver. *Musicophilia: Tales of Music and the Brain.* New York: Alfred A. Knopf, 2007.

Sadie, Stanley. *The New Grove: Dictionary of Music and Musicians.* London: Macmillan, 1980.

Seroff, Victor. *Sergei Prokofiev; a Soviet Tragedy.* New York: Funk & Wagnalls, 1968.

Shanet, Howard. *Philharmonic: A History of New York's Orchestra.* New York: Doubleday, 1975.

Sherrin, Ned. *The Oxford Dictionary of Humorous Quotations.* 3rd ed. Oxford: Oxford University Press, 2005.

Slonimsky, Nicolas. *Music since 1900.* New York: Schirmer, 1994.

Slonimsky, Nicolas. *Perfect Pitch: A Life Story*. Oxford: Oxford University Press, 1988.

Slonimsky, Nicolas. *A Thing or Two about Music*. New York: Allen, Towne & Heath, 1948.

Spiegl, Fritz. *Fritz Spiegl's Book of Musical Blunders and Other Musical Curiosities*. London: Robson, 1996.

Spiegl, Fritz. *Lives, Wives, and Loves of the Great Composers*. London: M. Boyars, 1997.

Straus, Joseph Nathan. *Extraordinary Measures: Disability in Music*. Oxford: Oxford University Press, 2011.

Stravinsky, Igor and Robert Craft. *Themes and Episodes*. New York: Alfred A. Knopf, 1967.

Stuckenschmidt, Hans Heinz. *Maurice Ravel; Variations on His Life and Work*. Philadelphia: Chilton Book, 1968.

Swan, Alfred J. *Scriabin*. New York: Da Capo, 1969.

"Steel Strike Opera Is Put Off by WPA." *New York Times*, June 17, 1937.

Tchaikovsky, Peter I. (Wladimir Lakond, translator). *The Diaries of Tchaikovsky*. New York: W.W. Norton & Co, 1945.

Vishnevskaya, Galina. *Galina: A Russian Story*. San Diego: Harcourt Brace Jovanovich, 1984.

Wade-Matthews, Max. *Encyclopedia of Music: Instruments of the Orchestra*. London: Southwater, 2010.

Walsh, Stephen. *Stravinsky: The Second Exile: France and America, 1934-1971*. New York: Alfred A. Knopf, 2006.

Watson, Derek. *The Wordsworth Dictionary of Musical Quotations*. Edinburgh: Wordsworth Reference, 1994.

Werfel, Alma Mahler, and E.B. Ashton. *And the Bridge Is Love*. New York: Harcourt, Brace, 1958.

Werth, Alexander. *Musical Uproar in Moscow*. London: Turnstile, 1949.

Whiteman, Paul. *An Experiment in Modern Music: Paul Whiteman at Aeolian Hall*. Smithsonian Collection, 1981. Vinyl recording.

Wikipedia. Wikimedia Foundation, N.d. Web. <https://www.wikipedia.org/>.

Zimmerman, Franklin B. *Henry Purcell, 1659-1695: His Life and Times*. Philadelphia: University of Pennsylvania Press, 1983.

Coda

About the Author

I was born, raised, and educated in Detroit, Michigan. Coming from a Polish-American family, it was mandatory that I study the accordion and I began playing professionally at Polish weddings at the age of eleven. I became hooked on music in junior high school, where I encountered an extraordinary music teacher, Annabella Miller. I attended Cass Technical High School, majoring in music and playing tuba and string bass in band and orchestra and singing tenor in the choir. Recognizing my laziness, I decided not to pursue a performance degree. Upon graduation from Wayne State University with a degree in music theory, I decided to become a music librarian, following the lead of two mentors, Bruno Nettl, then music librarian at Wayne State and Kurtz Myers, head of the performing arts division at the Detroit Public Library. I earned a master's degree in library science from the University of Michigan and joined the staff of the Library of Congress in 1964, where I served for twenty-five years, not as a music librarian but as an administrator.

My passion for music never subsided. I describe myself as a "professional listener." It is not unusual to attend four concerts a week. After retiring I have travelled the world attending concerts and opera, visiting music monuments and museums, and the grave sites of famous composers and musicians. In over six decades I've amassed a sizable collection of autographs of musicians and composers, art work and a stamp collection with music subjects.

I have had the pleasure of singing with choirs which got me onto Carnegie Hall and the Kennedy Center stages, the Viennese cathedral Stephansdom and Venice's San Marco Basilica. With the Washington Chorus I participated in the recordings of Mussorgsky's opera *Boris Godunov* and Shostakovich's *Babi Yar* symphony, both under the direction of Mistislav Rostropovich. I have played the pianos of George Gershwin, Scott Joplin, Edvard Grieg,

Liberace, Cole Porter, and Percy Grainger and the White House and Supreme Court pianos.

In retirement I have served on the board of the American Music Research Center (University of Colorado, Boulder), the Boulder Bach Festival, the Greater Boulder Youth Orchestras, and the Colorado Music Festival. For the latter I chaired its search committee for a new music director in 2012. Most recently I commissioned American Carter Pann to compose his third string quartet for the Ajax String Quartet.

In 2015 I published a memoir, *Polkas and Pierogies*. It is available on Kindle.

Arthur J. Lieb
Boulder, Colorado
November 2017

Made in the USA
Columbia, SC
23 July 2023